Consider THE Blessings

Consider the Blessings

TRUE ACCOUNTS OF GOD'S HAND IN OUR LIVES

THOMAS S. MONSON

DESERET
BOOK

SALT LAKE CITY, UTAH

Library of Congress Cataloging-in-Publication Data
(CIP on file)
ISBN 978-1-60907-716-7

Printed in the United States of America
Worzalla Publishing Company, Stevens Point, WI

10   9   8   7   6   5   4   3   2   1

CONTENTS

PREFACE

IN OCTOBER 1963, Thomas S. Monson became the newest member of the Quorum of the Twelve Apostles of The Church of Jesus Christ of Latter-day Saints. Elder Monson soon endeared himself to congregations throughout the world with his capacity to draw meaningful lessons out of life's experiences. The warm, memorable true accounts he has shared over the years have become a hallmark of his teaching style.

In commemoration of President Monson's fiftieth anniversary as an Apostle, Deseret Book is pleased to offer this beautifully illustrated collection of fifty of those true accounts, created in a way that will make them easy to share with the whole family and in other settings where an inspiring example might set the stage for a meaningful gospel discussion.

Each of these accounts helps us understand how intimately involved our Father in Heaven is in our lives, how much He cares for us, and how much He needs us to be there for one another. As we consider the blessings He has bestowed on us, we will be filled with gratitude. Then, as we follow the example of our prophet in reaching out to help and serve each other, the examples we create in our own lives will be an inspiration for generations to come.

FOR MANY YEARS my assignments took me into that part of Germany which was behind what was called the Iron Curtain. Under Communist control, those who lived in that area of Germany had lost nearly all of their freedoms. Activities of our youth were restricted; all actions were monitored.

two sticks of gum

Shortly after I assumed my responsibilities for that area, I attended a most uplifting conference held in that part of Germany. Following the inspirational songs and spoken word, I felt the impression to meet briefly outside of the old building with the precious teenage youth. They were relatively few in number but listened to every word I spoke. They had hungered for the word and encouragement of an Apostle of the Lord.

Prior to attending the conference, before leaving the United States, I had felt the prompting to buy three cartons of chewing gum. I purchased three flavors: Doublemint, Spearmint, and Juicy Fruit. Now, as the gathering of the youth was concluded, I distributed carefully to each youth two sticks of gum—something they had never before tasted. They received the gift with joy.

The years went by. I returned to Dresden—the site of our earlier conference. Now we had chapels; now the people had freedom. Germany was no longer separated by political boundaries but had become one nation. The youth were now adults with children of their own.

Following a large and inspirational conference, a mother and her daughter sought me out to speak to me. The daughter said to me, "President Monson, do you remember long ago holding a brief gathering of youth following a district conference, where you gave to each boy and each girl two sticks of chewing gum?"

I responded, "Yes, I surely do remember."

She continued, "My mother was one to whom you gave that gift. She told me that she rationed in little pieces one stick of gum. She mentioned how sweet to the taste it was and so precious to her." Then, under the approving smile of her dear mother, she handed to me a small box. As I opened the lid of the box, there I beheld the other stick of gum, still with its wrapper after nearly twenty years. "My mother and I want you to have this," she said.

The tears flowed, embraces followed. The mother then spoke to me: "Before you came to our conference so many years ago, I had prayed to my Heavenly Father to know that He indeed cared about me. I saved that gift so that I might remember and teach my daughter that Heavenly Father does hear our prayers."

I still have in my possession that gift—even a symbol of faith and assurance of the heavenly help our Father and His Son, Jesus Christ, will provide. 🌿

a bright spot
on their souls

ONE EVENING YEARS AGO, as I went home teaching, I saw a member of our ward, a wonderful retired high priest, out in bad weather with a little pail trying to obtain a few lumps of coal from his uncovered coal pile. I helped him fill the pail, and then we took it inside and attempted to start a fire in the stove of that cold house. I said, "John, how long have you had wet coal?"

He replied, "Bishop, I've never had dry coal in the winter." That worried me.

Later that evening, as I pondered and meditated, I thought of another member of our ward who was temporarily unemployed—a carpenter who had a furnace that ate coal slack as though it were going out of style. He was too proud to ask for help from the welfare program. Suddenly the pieces came together. I telephoned him and said, "Reeves, we need you to build a coal house, but I won't let you do it unless you permit me to deliver four tons of slack to your house from the Deseret Coal Mine."

He said, "Well, if you put it that way, I'll do it."

Now, where were we to obtain the materials? I approached the proprietors of a local lumberyard from whom we frequently purchased products. I remember saying to the men, "How would the two of you like to paint a bright spot on your souls this winter day?" Not knowing exactly what I meant, they agreed readily. They were invited to donate the lumber and hardware for the coal shed.

Within days the project was completed. I was invited to inspect the outcome. The coal shed was simply beautiful in its sleek covering of battleship gray paint. The carpenter, who was a high priest, testified that he had actually felt inspired as he labored on this modest shed. My older friend, with obvious appreciation, stroked the wall of the sturdy structure. He pointed out to me the wide door, the shiny hinges; and then he opened to my view the supply of dry coal that filled the shed. In a voice filled with emotion, he said, in words I shall ever treasure, "Bishop, take a look at the finest coal shed a man ever had." Its beauty was surpassed only by the pride in the builder's heart.

And the elderly recipient labored each weekday at the ward chapel, dusting the benches, vacuuming the carpet runners, and arranging the hymnbooks. He, too, worked for that which he had received. 🌿

IN 2004, a 9-plus magnitude undersea earthquake struck off the coast of Sumatra, generating tsunamis that took the lives of nearly 300,000 people. The day after the tsunami hit, Elder Subandriyo, an Area Seventy living in Indonesia, called upon several Saints he knew he could trust. One call he made was to the district Young Women president, Bertha Suranto. He asked her to purchase the materials for three thousand hygiene kits. Then he asked her to help make arrangements for volunteers to unload a cargo plane.

you are our brothers and sisters

A few days later, Sister Suranto volunteered to travel to the areas hardest hit by the tsunami. En route, she first stopped off in the northern Sumatra city of Medan, where she immediately began purchasing building materials, tents, food, clothing, kitchen stoves, school uniforms, and materials for thousands of additional hygiene kits.

She reported, "When we had the option of buying cheap goods or quality goods, we bought quality. If we wouldn't wear or use something ourselves, we didn't buy it."

Sister Suranto joined other members of the Church who worked from early morning until late at night filling more than forty trucks, each forty feet long, with tens of thousands of needed items. As each truck was filled, Bertha phoned ahead to her husband, who was with another group of Saints in Banda Aceh, one of the hardest hit areas. He received the trucks his wife had filled and helped to distribute the items among those in need—99 percent of whom were Muslim.

In many cases the boxes—each labeled, "A Gift from The Church of Jesus Christ of Latter-day Saints"—were stacked inside the mosques. Everywhere our volunteers went, townspeople ran out to greet and welcome them. "We felt as though we were movie stars," Sister Suranto said. "Often we arrived in villages, towns, and refugee camps that had not received help from anyone else."

Each time they met with village leaders, they asked, "What is it you most need?" One village chief said that, more than anything else, his village needed copies of the Koran because theirs had been swept away in the tsunami. A few days later, the Church presented the village with seven hundred copies of the Koran.

As trucks from the Church were unloaded into mosques and city squares, the word rang out, "We have received another donation from the Jesus Church!" And hundreds of grateful mothers, fathers, and children lined up to receive the life-sustaining goods. Heads of villages and heads of families smiled whenever Sister Suranto and the other members of the Church came. "You are a different church," they said. "You don't want anything in return—only to serve. You are our brothers and sisters."

As for Sister Suranto, her outlook on life changed as well. She said, "Before the tsunami, I didn't want to associate with those of other faiths. The people we helped probably felt the same way. Very few of them had ever heard of our Church or knew anything about us. We were strangers to each other. Today, things are different. Today, we feel a close bond. We know we are brothers and sisters."

I'll be there

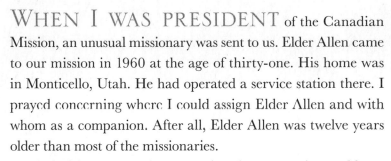

WHEN I WAS PRESIDENT of the Canadian Mission, an unusual missionary was sent to us. Elder Allen came to our mission in 1960 at the age of thirty-one. His home was in Monticello, Utah. He had operated a service station there. I prayed concerning where I could assign Elder Allen and with whom as a companion. After all, Elder Allen was twelve years older than most of the missionaries.

A decision was made concerning the companion and location. After a few weeks, I spoke to Elder Allen's companion and queried, "How do the two of you get along?"

The answer from a nineteen-year-old companion tells it all: "He is the best and most dedicated missionary I have ever known. Each morning he's up cooking a modest breakfast before my eyes are half open. After having completed our morning study, he's found standing at the door, ready to go forth and serve." Elder Allen was modest—even shy—but filled with faith. Many were those he led to truth.

Years later, visiting at Elder Allen's bedside just prior to his passing beyond the veil, I learned from his family about this silent servant of God. His father left the family when Elder Allen was only five or six years of age. Since his mother was an invalid, he was raised by his grandmother and two aunts. When he was seventeen, his mother passed away. After graduating from high school, he served for a time in the army. When he

returned home, he became the sole support for his two aunts, but his great desire was to serve a mission. Determined to go, he worked very hard for many years to save the money. He saved enough money to have a home built for his aunts, as well as providing a two-year supply of food for them so that they would be taken care of while he served. He also saved all the money necessary for his mission. I feel honored to have had him serve in the Canadian Mission.

In the hospital room was Elder Allen's dear wife, Colleen, and their precious children. We reminisced about missionary days and cherished experiences. There was laughter. There were tears. A son and sons-in-law joined me in providing a priesthood blessing. The Holy Spirit filled the hospital room. To keep from weeping, I touched his hand and asked, "Harold, what do you think of the temple under construction in Monticello?"

He replied softly, "Well, President, I love Monticello, and there is no place I would rather be than there at the time the temple is dedicated. President, I'll be there—if not in person, then surely in spirit."

Quietly, but knowingly, I assured him, "Yes, Elder Allen, you will be there."

May we "be there" in the celestial kingdom of our God and hear from Him the greeting, "Well done, thou good and faithful servant: thou hast been faithful over a few things, I will make thee ruler over many things: enter thou into the joy of thy lord" (Matthew 25:21). 🌿

WHEN I WAS APPROACHING

my eighteenth birthday, my friends and I were all
very fearful. World War II had not as yet concluded,
and every young man knew that he had to make a
choice. He did not have much latitude in the choice.
He could choose to go in the army, or he could
choose to go in the navy. I enlisted in the navy.

a choice to make

As forty-four of us young men stood there in the recruiting office, I will never forget the chief petty officers coming up to us with a choice. They said, "Now, you young men have two choices to make. On one hand, you can be wise and you can choose to join the regular navy. You can enlist for four years. You will be in receipt of the finest schooling. You will be given every opportunity because the navy looks upon you as its own. If you choose not to follow this direction, you can take the naval reserves. The navy does not have much interest in the naval reserves at this stage of the game. You will receive no schooling. You will be sent out to sea duty. Who knows what your future might be."

Then they asked us to sign on the dotted line. I turned to my father and I said, "What should I do, Dad?" The tears were falling from his eyes. He said, "I don't know anything about the navy." That was the same position every father was in that day as his son tried to make a choice.

Forty-two out of the forty-four joined the regular navy for four years. The forty-third one could not pass the regular navy physical, so he had to enlist in the reserves. As they came to me, I want to confess to you that I let a prayer go heavenward from my soul, and I was earnestly hoping that the Lord would answer it, and He did. The thought came to me just as clear as though I had seen a vision, "Ask those chief petty officers how they chose." I asked each one of those veteran petty officers, "Did you choose the regular navy, or did you choose the reserves?" Every single one of them had chosen the reserves.

I turned to them and I said, "With all the wisdom and experience that you have, I want to be on your side." I chose the reserves, which meant that I enlisted for the duration of the war plus six months. The war ended, and within a year I was honorably discharged from the service. I was able to pursue my education. I had the privilege of serving as a member of a bishopric. Who knows how my life might have been changed had I not taken the moment that it required to call upon my Heavenly Father for guidance and direction in what might appear to some to be a minor decision. ❧

silent night,
holy night

WHEN I SERVED as a bishop, there resided
in our ward a young man, Frank, who, as a deacon, led a
successful rescue of three lovely women who were in need.
In the neighborhood there lived many elderly widows of
limited means. All the year long, Frank and his fellow dea-
cons saved and planned for a glorious Christmas party.
They were thinking of themselves—until the Christmas
spirit prompted them to think of others. Frank, as their
leader, suggested to his companions that the funds they
had accumulated so carefully be used not for the planned
party but rather for the benefit of three elderly widows
who resided together. The boys made their plans. As their
bishop, I needed but to follow.

With the enthusiasm of a new adventure, the boys
purchased a giant roasting chicken, the potatoes, the vege-
tables, the cranberries, and all that comprises the tradi-
tional Christmas feast. To the widows' home they went
carrying their gifts of treasure. Through the snow and up
the path to the tumbledown porch they came. A knock at
the door, the sound of slow footsteps, and then they met.

In the unmelodic voices characteristic of thirteen-
year-olds, the boys sang "Silent night, holy night; all is
calm, all is bright." They then presented their gifts. Angels
on that glorious night of long ago sang no more beautifully,
nor did wise men present gifts of greater meaning.

the binding balm

ONE OF THE SAD FACTS of life is that there are mothers and fathers, sons and daughters, who have, through thoughtless comment, isolated themselves from one another. An account of how such a tragedy was narrowly averted occurred in the life of a lad we shall call Jack.

True account

Throughout Jack's life, he and his father had many serious arguments. One day, when he was seventeen, they had a particularly violent one. Jack said to his father: "This is the straw that breaks the camel's back. I'm leaving home, and I shall never return." So saying, he went into the house and packed a bag. His mother begged him to stay, but he was too angry and upset to listen. He left her crying at the doorway.

As he left the yard and was about to pass through the gate, he heard his father call to him: "Jack, I know that a large share of the blame for your leaving rests with me. For this I am deeply sorry. But I want you to know that if you should ever wish to return to our home, you'll always be welcome. And I'll try to be a better father to you. I want you to know that I'll always love you."

Jack said nothing, but went to the bus station and bought a ticket to a distant point. As he sat in the bus watching the miles go by, he commenced to think about the words of his father. He began to realize how much love it had required for his father to do what he had done. Dad had apologized. He had invited Jack back and had left the words ringing in the summer air, "I love you."

Jack realized that the next move was up to him. He knew that the only way he could ever find peace with himself was to demonstrate to his father the same kind of maturity, goodness, and love that Dad had demonstrated toward him. Jack got off the bus. He bought a return ticket home and went back.

He arrived shortly before midnight. He entered the house and turned on the light. There in the rocking chair sat his father, his head in his hands. As he looked up and saw Jack, he rose from the chair and they rushed into each other's arms. Jack often said, "Those last years that I was home were among the happiest of my life."

We could say, Here was a boy who overnight became a man. Here was a father who, suppressing passion and bridling pride, rescued his son before he became one of that vast "lost battalion" resulting from fractured families and shattered homes. Love was the binding balm. Love—so often felt; so seldom expressed.

AS A BISHOP, I worried about any members who were less active, not attending, not serving. Such was my thought one day as I drove down the street where Ben and Emily Fullmer lived. Aches and pains of advancing years had caused them to withdraw from activity to the shelter of their home—isolated, detached, shut out from the mainstream of daily life and association. Ben and Emily had not been in our sacrament meeting for many years. Ben, a former bishop, would sit in his front room reading the New Testament.

Heavenly Father knows

I was en route from my uptown sales office to our plant on Industrial Road. For some reason I had driven down First West, a street I never had traveled before to reach the destination of our plant. Then I felt the unmistakable prompting to park my car and visit Ben and Emily, even though I was on my way to a meeting. I did not heed the impression at first but drove on for two more blocks; however, when the impression came again, I returned to their home.

It was a sunny weekday afternoon. I approached the door to their home and knocked. I heard the tiny fox terrier bark at my approach. Emily welcomed me in. Upon seeing me, she exclaimed, "All day long I have waited for my phone to ring. It has been silent. I hoped that the postman would deliver a letter. He brought only bills. Bishop, how did you know today is my birthday?"

I answered, "God knows, Emily, for He loves you."

In the quiet of their living room, I said to Ben and Emily, "I don't know why I was directed here today, but our Heavenly Father knows. Let's kneel in prayer and ask Him why." This we did, and the answer came. As we arose from our knees, I said to Brother Fullmer, "Ben, would you come to priesthood meeting and relate to our Aaronic Priesthood youth the story you once told me of how you and a group of boys were en route to the Jordan River to swim one Sunday, but you felt the Spirit direct you to attend Sunday School. One of the boys who failed to respond to that Spirit drowned that Sunday. Our boys would like to hear your testimony."

"I'll do it," he responded.

I then said to Sister Fullmer, "Emily, I know you have a beautiful voice. My mother has told me so. Our ward conference is a few weeks away, and our choir will sing. Would you join the choir and attend our ward conference and perhaps sing a solo?"

"What will the number be?" she inquired.

"I don't know," I said, "but I'd like you to sing it."

She sang. He spoke. Hearts were gladdened by the return to activity of Ben and Emily. They rarely missed a sacrament meeting from that day forward. The language of the Spirit had been spoken. It had been heard. It had been understood. Hearts were touched and souls saved. Ben and Emily Fullmer had come home.

thank you for
being kind

WHEN I WAS A DEACON, I loved baseball. In fact, I still do. I had a fielder's glove inscribed with the name *Mel Ott*. He was the premiere player of my day. My friends and I would play ball in a small alleyway behind the houses where we lived. Our playing field was cramped but all right, provided you hit straight away to center field. However, if you hit the ball to the right of center, disaster was at the door.

Here lived Mrs. Shinas, who, from her kitchen window, would watch us play. As soon as a stray ball rolled to her porch, her large dog would retrieve the ball and present it to her as she opened the door. Into her house Mrs. Shinas would return and add the ball to the many she had previously confiscated. She was our nemesis, the destroyer of our fun—even the bane of our existence. None of us had a good word for Mrs. Shinas, but we had plenty of bad words for her. None of us would speak to her, and she never spoke to us. She was hampered by a stiff leg that impaired her walking and must have caused her great pain. She and her husband had no children, lived secluded lives, and rarely came out of their house.

This private war continued for some time—and then an inspired thaw melted the ice of winter and brought a springtime of good feelings to the stalemate.

One evening as I performed my daily task of watering our front lawn, holding the nozzle of the hose in hand as was the style at that time, I noticed that Mrs. Shinas's lawn was dry and beginning to turn brown. I honestly don't know what came over me, but I took a few more minutes and, with our hose, watered her lawn. I continued to do this throughout the summer, and then when autumn came, I hosed her lawn free of leaves as I did ours and stacked the leaves in piles at the street's edge to be burned or gathered. During the entire summer I had not seen Mrs. Shinas. We boys had long since given up playing ball in the alleyway. We had run out of baseballs and had no money to buy more.

Early one evening, Mrs. Shinas's front door opened, and she beckoned for me to jump the small fence and come to her front porch. This I did, and as I approached her, she invited me into her living room, where I was asked to sit in a comfortable chair. She treated me to cookies and milk. Then she went to the kitchen and returned with a large box filled with baseballs and softballs, representing several seasons of her confiscation efforts. The filled box was presented to me. The treasure, however, was not to be found in the gift, but rather in her words. I saw for the first time a smile come across the face of Mrs. Shinas, and she said, "Tommy, I want you to have these baseballs, and I want to thank you for being kind to me." I expressed my own gratitude to her and walked from her home a better boy than when I entered. No longer were we enemies. Now we were friends. The "Golden Rule" had again succeeded.

this morning
we're not hungry

WHEN I SERVED as a mission president, my wife and I became intimately acquainted with almost four hundred missionaries. We had one young missionary, Elder Davidson, who had become very ill. After he had been hospitalized for weeks, it was evident that he would need an extremely serious and complicated surgery.

The surgeon asked that we send for the missionary's mother and father before he undertook the operation. He said there was a great likelihood that Elder Davidson could not survive the surgery. The parents came, and late that evening his father and I, in that hospital room in Toronto, Canada, placed our hands upon the head of that young missionary and gave him a blessing. What happened following that blessing was a testimony to me.

Elder Davidson was in a six-bed ward in the hospital. The other beds were occupied by five men with a variety of illnesses. The morning of Elder Davidson's surgery, his bed was empty. The nurse came into the room with the breakfast these husky men normally ate. She carried a tray to bed number one and said, "Fried eggs this morning, and I have an extra portion for you." Bed number one was occupied by a man who was lying on his bed with his toe wrapped up in a bandage. He had suffered an accident with his lawn mower. Other than his injured toe, he was well physically. He said to the nurse, "I'll not be eating this morning."

"All right, we shall give your breakfast to your partner in bed number two!" As she went over to him, he said, "No, I think I'll not eat this morning." She said, "That's two in a row. I don't understand you men, and there is no one this morning in bed three." She went on to bed four, bed five, and bed six, and the answer was the same: "No, this morning we're not hungry."

The young lady put her hands on her hips and said, "Every other morning you eat us out of house and home and today not one of you wants to eat. What is the reason?"

And then the man who occupied bed number six came forth with the answer. He said, "You see, bed number three is empty. Our friend, Davidson, is in the operating room under the surgeon's hands. He needs all the help he can get. He is a missionary for his church; and while he has been lying on that bed while we have been patients in this ward, he has talked to us about the principles of his church—principles of prayer, of faith, and of fasting wherein we call upon the Lord for blessings." He said, "We don't know much about the Mormon church, but we have learned a great deal about Davidson; and we are fasting for him today."

I might tell you that the operation was a success. In fact, when I attempted to pay the surgeon, he countered, "Why, that would be dishonest for me to accept a fee. I have never before performed surgery when my hands seemed to be guided by a power which was other than my own. No," he said, "I wouldn't take a fee for the surgery which someone on high helped me to perform."

the Lord made
up the difference

AT THE CULTURAL CELEBRATION for the Kansas City Temple, something occurred that had an impact on hundreds. As with so much that happens in our lives, at the time it seemed to be just another experience where everything worked out. However, as I learned of the circumstances associated with the cultural celebration the evening before the temple was dedicated, I realized that the performance that night was not ordinary. Rather, it was quite remarkable.

As with all cultural events held in conjunction with temple dedications, the youth in the Kansas City Missouri Temple district had rehearsed the performance in separate groups in their own areas. The plan was that they would meet all together in the large rented municipal center on the Saturday morning of the performance so that they could learn when and where to enter, where they were to stand, how much space should be between them and the person next to them, how to exit the main floor, and so forth—many details which they would have to grasp during the day as those in charge put the various scenes together so that the final performance would be polished and professional.

There was just one major problem that day. The entire production was dependent on prerecorded segments that would be shown on the large screen known as a Jumbotron. These recorded segments were critical to the entire production. They not only tied it all together, but each televised segment would introduce the next performance. The video segments provided the framework on which the entire production depended. And the Jumbotron was not working.

Technicians worked frantically to solve the problem while the youth waited, hundreds of them, losing precious rehearsal time. The situation began to look impossible.

Just an hour before the audience would begin to enter the center, three thousand youth knelt on the floor and prayed together. They prayed that those working on the Jumbotron would be inspired to know what to do to repair it; they asked their Heavenly Father to make up for what they themselves could not do because of the shortage of time.

Soon after this prayer was offered, one of the technicians came to tell them that the Jumbotron was finally working. He attributed this to luck, but all those youth knew better.

When we entered the municipal center that evening, we had no idea of the difficulties of the day. Only later did we learn of them. What we witnessed, however, was a beautiful, polished performance—one of the best I have seen. The youth radiated a glorious, powerful spirit which was felt by all who were present. They seemed to know just where to enter, where to stand, and how to interact with all the other performers around them. When I learned that their rehearsals had been cut short and that many of the numbers had not been rehearsed by the entire group, I was astonished. No one would have known. The Lord had indeed made up the difference.

I learned later that a few months following the cultural celebration, an ad hoc member of the cultural celebration committee, Eric Webster, who is also a professional audio engineer in the Kansas City area, had an opportunity to work again with the same technicians who had worked on the Jumbotron during the celebration. They told Eric that they still had no idea why the Jumbotron worked that night because they realized, as they took it down after the celebration was over, that the parts on the Jumbotron were incompatible. The Jumbotron should never have worked in the first place.

I never cease to be amazed by how the Lord can motivate and direct the length and breadth of His kingdom and yet have time to provide inspiration concerning one individual—or one cultural celebration or one Jumbotron. The fact that He can, that He does, is a testimony to me. 🍃

WHEN I WAS FIRST CALLED as a bishop, I discovered that our record for subscriptions to the *Relief Society Magazine* in the Sixth-Seventh Ward had been at a low ebb. Prayerfully we analyzed the names of the individuals whom we could call to be magazine representative. The inspiration dictated that Elizabeth Keachie should be given the assignment. As her bishop, I approached her with the task. She responded, "Bishop Monson, I'll do it."

Elizabeth Keachie was of Scottish descent, and when she replied, "I'll do it," one knew she indeed would. She and her sister-in-law, Helen Ivory—neither more than five feet tall—commenced to walk the ward, house by house, street by street, and block by block. The result was phenomenal. We had more subscriptions to the *Relief Society Magazine* than had been recorded by all the other units of the stake combined.

I congratulated Elizabeth Keachie one Sunday evening and said to her, "Your task is done."

She replied, "Not yet, Bishop. There are two square blocks we have not yet covered."

When she told me which blocks they were, I said, "Sister Keachie, no one lives on those blocks. They are totally industrial."

"Just the same," she said, "I'll feel better if Nell and I go and check them ourselves."

On a rainy day, she and Nell covered those final two blocks. On the first one, she found no home, nor did she on the second. She and

Sister Ivory paused, however, at a driveway that was muddy from the recent storm. Sister Keachie gazed down the driveway, which was adjacent to a machine shop, perhaps a hundred feet and there noticed a garage. This was not a normal garage, however, in that there was a curtain at the window.

She turned to her companion and said, "Nell, shall we go and investigate?"

The two sweet sisters then walked down the muddy driveway forty feet to a point where the entire view of the garage could be seen. Now they noticed a door that had been cut into the side of the garage, which door was unseen from the street. They also noticed that there was a chimney with smoke rising from it.

Elizabeth Keachie knocked at the door. A man sixty-eight years of age, William Ringwood, answered. They then presented their story concerning the need of every home having the *Relief Society Magazine*. William Ringwood replied, "You'd better ask my father." Ninety-four-year-old Charles W. Ringwood then came to the door and also listened to the message. He subscribed.

Elizabeth Keachie reported to me the presence of these two men in our ward. When I requested their membership certificates from Church headquarters, I received a call from the membership department at the Presiding Bishopric's Office. The clerk said, "Are you sure you have living in your ward Charles W. Ringwood?"

I replied that I did, whereupon she reported that the membership certificate for him had remained in the "lost and unknown" file of the Presiding Bishopric's Office for the previous sixteen years.

On Sunday morning Elizabeth Keachie and Nell Ivory brought to our priesthood meeting Charles and William Ringwood. This was the first time they had been inside a chapel for many years. Charles Ringwood was the oldest deacon I had ever met. His son was the oldest male member holding no priesthood I had ever met.

It became my opportunity to ordain Brother Charles Ringwood a teacher and then a priest and finally an elder. I shall never forget his interview with respect to seeking a temple recommend. He handed me a silver dollar which he took from an old, worn leather coin purse and said, "This is my fast offering."

I said, "Brother Ringwood, you owe no fast offering. You need it yourself."

"I want to receive the blessings, not retain the money," he responded.

It was my opportunity to take Charles Ringwood to the Salt Lake Temple and to attend with him the endowment session.

Within a few months, Charles W. Ringwood passed away. At his funeral service, I noticed his family sitting on the front rows in the mortuary chapel, but I noticed also two sweet women sitting near the rear of the chapel, Elizabeth Keachie and Helen Ivory.

As I gazed upon those two faithful and dedicated women and contemplated their personal influence for good, the promise of the Lord filled my very soul: "I, the Lord, am merciful and gracious unto those who fear me, and delight to honor those who serve me in righteousness and in truth unto the end. Great shall be their reward and eternal shall be their glory" (Doctrine and Covenants 76:5–6).

STAN, a dear friend of mine, was taken seriously ill and rendered partially paralyzed. He had been robust in health, athletic in build, and active in many pursuits. Now he was unable to walk or to stand. His wheelchair was his home. The finest of physicians had cared for him, and the prayers of family and friends offered in a spirit of hope and trust. Yet Stan continued to lie in the confinement of his bed at the University Hospital. He despaired.

never postpone a prompting

Late one afternoon I was swimming at the Deseret Gym, gazing at the ceiling while backstroking width after width. Silently, but ever so clearly, there came to my mind the thought: "Here you swim almost effortlessly, while your friend Stan languishes in his hospital bed, unable to move." I felt the prompting: "Get to the hospital and give him a blessing."

I ceased my swimming, dressed, and hurried to Stan's room at the hospital. His bed was empty. A nurse said he was in his wheelchair at the swimming pool, preparing for therapy. I hurried to the area, and there was Stan, all alone, at the edge of the deeper portion of the pool. We greeted one another and returned to his room, where a priesthood blessing was provided.

Slowly but surely, strength and movement returned to Stan's legs. First he could stand on faltering feet. Then he learned once again to walk—step by step. No one would have known that Stan had lain so close to death and with no hope of recovery.

Frequently Stan spoke in Church meetings and told of the goodness of the Lord to him. To some he revealed the dark thoughts of depression that engulfed him that afternoon as he sat in his wheelchair at the edge of the pool, sentenced, it seemed, to a life of despair. He told how he pondered the alternative. It would be so easy to propel the hated wheelchair into the silent water of the deep pool. Life would then be over. But at that precise moment he saw me, his friend. That day Stan learned literally that we do not walk alone. I, too, learned a lesson that day: Never, never, never postpone following a prompting. 🦋

you must be
a Mormon

MANY YEARS AGO I boarded a plane in San Francisco en route to Los Angeles. As I sat down, the seat next to mine was empty. Soon, however, there occupied that seat a most lovely young lady. As the plane became airborne, I noticed that she was reading a book. As one is wont to do, I glanced at the title: *A Marvelous Work and a Wonder.* I mustered up my courage and said to her, "You must be a Mormon."

She replied, "Oh no. Why would you ask?"

I said, "Well, you're reading a book written by LeGrand Richards, a very prominent member of The Church of Jesus Christ of Latter-day Saints."

She responded, "Is that right? A friend gave this to me, but I don't know much about it. However, it has aroused my curiosity."

I wondered silently, *Should I be forward and say more about the Church?* The words of the Apostle Peter crossed my mind: "Be ready always to give an answer to every [one] that asketh you a reason of the hope that is in you" (1 Peter 3:15). I decided that now was the time for me to share my testimony with her. I told her that it had been my privilege years before to assist Elder Richards in printing *A Marvelous Work and a Wonder.* I told her of the great missionary spirit of this man. I also told her of the many thousands of people who had embraced the truth after reading that which he had prepared. Then it was my privilege, all the way to Los Angeles, to answer her questions relative to the Church—intelligent questions that came from her heart, which I perceived was seeking the truth. I asked if I might have the opportunity to have the missionaries call upon her. I asked if she would like to attend one of our wards in San Francisco. Her answers were affirmative. She gave me her name and indicated that she was a flight attendant on her way to an assignment.

Upon returning home, I wrote to the mission president and the stake president, advising them of my conversation and that I had written to her and sent along some suggested reading. Incidentally, I suggested that rather than sending two elders to the pretty off-duty flight attendant and her flight attendant roommate, two sister missionaries be assigned to call.

Several months passed by. Then I received a telephone call from the stake president, who asked, "Brother Monson, do you remember sitting next to a flight attendant on a trip from San Francisco to Los Angeles early this fall?" I answered affirmatively. He continued, "I thought you would like to know that she has just become the most

recently baptized and confirmed member of the Church. She would like to speak with you."

A sweet voice came on the line: "Brother Monson, thank you for sharing with me your testimony. I am the happiest member of the Church in all the world."

As tears filled my eyes and gratitude to God enlarged my soul, I thanked her and commended her on her search for truth and, having found it, her decision to enter those waters which cleanse and purify and provide entrance to eternal life.

I sat silently for a few minutes after replacing the telephone receiver. The words of our Savior coursed through my mind: "And whoso receiveth you, there I will be also, for I will go before your face. I will be on your right hand and on your left, and my Spirit shall be in your hearts, and mine angels round about you, to bear you up" (Doctrine and Covenants 84:88). Such is the promise to all of us when we follow the counsel and obey the commandments of Jesus of Nazareth, our Savior and our King.

OVER THE YEARS I have heard and read testimonies too numerous to count, shared with me by individuals who testify of the reality of the Resurrection and who have received, in their hours of greatest need, the peace and comfort promised by the Savior.

One day I received a touching letter from a father of seven who wrote about his family, in particular his son Jason, who had become ill when eleven years of age. Over the next few years, Jason's illness recurred several times. This father told of Jason's positive attitude and sunny disposition, despite his health challenges. Jason received the Aaronic Priesthood at age twelve and, his father reported, "always willingly magnified his responsibilities with excellence, whether he felt well or not." He received his Eagle Scout award when he was fourteen years old.

Not long after Jason's fifteenth birthday, he was once again admitted to the hospital. On one of his visits to see Jason, his father found him with his eyes closed. Not knowing whether Jason was asleep or awake, he began talking softly to him. "Jason," he said, "I know you have been through a lot in your short life and that your current condition is difficult. Even though you have a giant battle ahead, I don't ever want you to lose your faith in Jesus Christ." He said he was startled as Jason immediately

called to serve

opened his eyes and said "Never!" in a clear, resolute voice. Jason then closed his eyes and said no more.

His father wrote: "In this simple declaration, Jason expressed one of the most powerful, pure testimonies of Jesus Christ that I have ever heard. . . . As his declaration of 'Never!' became imprinted on my soul that day, my heart filled with joy that my Heavenly Father had blessed me to be the father of such a tremendous and noble boy."

Although his family was expecting this to be just another routine hospitalization, Jason passed away less than two weeks later. An older brother and sister were serving missions at the time. Another brother, Kyle, had just received his mission call. In fact, the call had come earlier than expected, and on August 5, just a week before Jason's passing, the family gathered in his hospital room so that Kyle's mission call could be opened there and shared with the entire family.

In his letter to me, this father included a photograph of Jason in his hospital bed, with his big brother Kyle standing beside the bed, holding his mission call. This caption was written beneath the photograph: "Called to serve their missions together—on both sides of the veil." 🌿

ELDER ERICKSON

THE CHURCH OF
JESUS CHRIST
OF LATTER-DAY SAINTS

SOMETIMES IT TAKES many years for the Lord's purposes to become known. Such was the case with a seemingly small, potentially insignificant event in the life of Brother Edwin Q. Cannon Jr. Brother Cannon was a missionary to Germany in 1938, where he loved the people and served faithfully. At the conclusion of his mission, he returned home to Salt Lake City. He married and commenced his own business.

we left everything behind

Forty years passed by. One day Brother Cannon came to my office and said he had been pruning his missionary slides. Among those slides he had kept since his mission were several he could not specifically identify. Every time he had planned to discard them, he had been impressed to keep them, although he was at a loss as to why. They were photographs taken by Brother Cannon during his mission when he served in Stettin, Germany, and were of a family—a mother, a father, a small girl, and a small boy. He knew their surname was Berndt but could remember nothing more about them. He indicated that he understood there was a Berndt who was a Church leader in Germany, and he thought, although the possibility was remote, that this Berndt might have some connection with the Berndts who had lived in Stettin and who were depicted in the photographs. Before disposing of the slides, he thought he would check with me.

I told Brother Cannon I was leaving shortly for Berlin, where I anticipated that I would see Dieter Berndt, the leader he mentioned, and that I would show the slides to him to see if there were any relationship and if he wanted them. There was a possibility I would also see Brother Berndt's sister, who was married to Dietmar Matern, a stake president in Hamburg.

The Lord didn't even let me get to Berlin before His purposes were accomplished. I was in Zurich, Switzerland, boarding the flight to Berlin, when who should also board the plane but Dieter Berndt. He sat next to me, and I told him I had some old slides of people named Berndt from Stettin. I handed them to him and asked if he could identify those shown in the photographs. As he looked at them carefully, he began to weep. He said, "Our family lived in Stettin during the war. My father was killed when an Allied bomb struck the plant where he worked. Not long afterward, the Russians invaded Poland and the area of Stettin. My mother took my sister and me and fled from the advancing enemy. Everything had to be left behind, including any photographs we had. Brother Monson, I am the little boy pictured in these slides, and my sister is the little girl. The man and woman are our dear parents. Until today, I have had no photographs of our childhood in Stettin or of my father."

Wiping away my own tears, I told Brother Berndt the slides were his. He placed them carefully and lovingly in his briefcase.

A precious blessing was bestowed that day because Brother Edwin Q. Cannon listened to a prompting and obeyed, though he knew not the reason why. 🦋

DURING THE FINAL PHASES

of World War II, I turned eighteen and was ordained an elder one week before I departed for active duty with the navy. A member of my ward bishopric was at the train station to bid me farewell. Just before train time, he placed two books into my hands.

it may come in handy

One was a popular satire in which I took interest. The other was entitled: *The Missionary Handbook.* I laughed and commented, "I'm not going on a mission." He answered, "Take it anyway—it may come in handy." It did. In basic training the quartermaster instructed us concerning how we might best pack our clothing in a large sea bag. He advised, "If you have some hard, rectangular object you can place in the bottom, your clothes will stay more firm." I suddenly remembered just the right rectangular object—*The Missionary Handbook.* Thus it served for sixteen weeks.

The night preceding our Christmas leave, our thoughts were, as always, on home. The quarters were quiet. Suddenly, I became aware that my buddy in the adjoining bunk, a Mormon boy, Leland Merrill, was moaning in pain. I asked, "What's the matter, Merrill?" He replied, "I'm sick. I'm *really sick.*" I advised him to go to the base dispensary, but he knowingly answered that such a course would prevent him from being home for Christmas.

The hours lengthened; his groans grew louder. Suddenly he whispered, "Monson, Monson, aren't you an elder?" I acknowledged this to be so, whereupon he asked, "Give me a blessing." Suddenly, I became very much aware that I had never given a blessing, I had never received such a blessing, I had never witnessed a blessing being given. My prayer to God was a plea for help. The answer came: "Look in the bottom of the sea bag." Thus, at two a.m., I spilled the contents of the bag on the deck, took the book to the night-light, and read how one blesses the sick. With about forty curious sailors looking on, I gave the shakiest blessing I've ever given. Before I could stow my gear, Leland Merrill was sleeping like a child.

The next morning Merrill smilingly turned to me and said: "Monson, I'm glad you hold the priesthood." His gladness was surpassed only by my joy. 🍃

SOME YEARS AGO a lovely young woman, Jami Palmer, then twelve years of age, was wheeled into my office by her parents. She had been diagnosed with cancer. Surgery would be required. The treatments would be many and the time of recovery long. It was a solemn moment as we visited. Father requested me to join him in blessing his crestfallen daughter, who had just had her dreams, her hopes, her plans placed on hold. All of us were weeping. The priesthood blessing was provided.

Jami underwent grueling and painful treatments for many months. By the time she had completed them, her cancer appeared to be in remission. Just a few years later, however, in one of her darkest hours, she learned that the cancer had returned and that she must again undergo months of chemotherapy, followed by a multiple-hour surgery to save her leg.

A long-planned hike with her Young Women class to the Timpanogos Cave was out of the question, she thought. Jami told her friends they would have to undertake the hike without her. Surely there was a catch in her voice and disappointment in her heart. But then the other Young Women responded emphatically, "No, Jami. You are going with us!"

"But I can't walk," came the anguished reply.

"Then, Jami, we'll carry you to the top." And they did, up and back.

None of those precious young women will ever forget that memorable day when, I am confident, a loving Heavenly Father looked down with a smile of approval and was well pleased. 🌿

a turning point

LATE ONE EVENING on a Pacific isle, a small boat slipped silently to its berth at the crude pier. Two Polynesian women helped Meli Mulipola from the boat and guided him to the well-worn pathway leading to the village road. The women marveled at the bright stars that twinkled in the midnight sky. The friendly moonlight guided them along their way. However, Meli Mulipola could not appreciate these delights of nature—the moon, the stars, the sky—for he was blind.

light in the darkness

His vision had been normal until that fateful day when, while he was working on a pineapple plantation, light turned suddenly to darkness and day became perpetual night. But he had learned of the Restoration of the gospel and the teachings of The Church of Jesus Christ of Latter-day Saints. His life had been brought into compliance with these teachings.

He and his loved ones had made this long voyage, having learned that one who held the priesthood of God was visiting among the islands. He sought a blessing under the hands of those who held the sacred priesthood. His wish was granted. Tears streamed from his sightless eyes and coursed down his brown cheeks, tumbling finally upon his native dress. He dropped to his knees and prayed, "Oh, God, Thou knowest I am blind. Thy servants have blessed me that if it be Thy will, my sight may return. Whether in Thy wisdom I see light or whether I see darkness all the days of my life, I will be eternally grateful for the truth of Thy gospel which I now see and which provides me the light of life."

He arose to his feet, thanked us for providing the blessing, and disappeared into the dark of the night. Silently he came; silently he departed. But his presence I shall never forget. I reflected upon the message of the Master, recorded in John 8:12, "I am the light of the world: he that followeth me shall not walk in darkness, but shall have the light of life." 🦋

square with
the Lord

LONG YEARS AGO, when I served as a bishop, I received notification that Mary Watson, a member of my ward, was a patient in the county hospital. When I went to visit her, I discovered her in a large room filled with so many beds that it was difficult to single her out. As I identified her bed and approached her, I said, "Hello, Mary."

She replied, "Hello, Bishop."

I noticed that a patient in the bed next to Mary Watson covered her face with the bedsheet.

I gave Mary Watson a blessing, shook her hand, and said good-bye, but I could not leave her side. It was as though an unseen hand were resting on my shoulder, and I felt within my soul that I was hearing these words: *Go over to the next bed where the little lady covered her face when you came in.* I did so. I have learned in my life never to postpone a prompting.

I approached the bedside of the other patient, gently tapped her shoulder, and carefully pulled back the sheet that had covered her face. Lo and behold! She too was a member of my ward. I had not known she was a patient in the hospital. Her name was Kathleen McKee. When her eyes met mine, she exclaimed through her tears, "Oh, Bishop, when you entered that door, I felt you had come to see me and bless me in response to my prayers. I was rejoicing inside to think that you would know I was here, but when you stopped at the other bed, my heart sank, and I knew that you had not come to see me."

I said to Kathleen McKee, "It does not matter that I didn't know you were here. It is important, however, that our Heavenly Father knew and that you had prayed silently for a priesthood blessing. It was He who prompted me to intrude on your privacy."

A blessing was given; a prayer was answered. I bestowed a kiss on her forehead and left the hospital with gratitude in my heart for the promptings of the Spirit. It would be the last time I was to see Kathleen McKee in mortality—but not the last time I heard from her.

Upon her death, the hospital called with this message: "Bishop Monson, Kathleen McKee died tonight. She made arrangements that we were to notify you, should she pass away. She left for you a key to her basement apartment."

Kathleen McKee had no immediate family. With my sweet wife accompanying me, I visited her humble apartment. I turned the key in the door, opened it, and switched on the light. There in her immaculate two-room apartment, I saw a small table with a note resting beneath an Alka-Seltzer bottle. The note, written in her own hand, said, "Bishop, my tithing is in this envelope, and the Alka-Seltzer bottle contains coins covering my fast offering. I am square with the Lord." The receipts were written.

I knew that the sweetness of that night would never be forgotten. Tears of gratitude to God filled my very soul for a faithful woman and a loving good-bye. 🍂

I SERVED AS A BISHOP during the period of the Korean War. We had received from Church headquarters a letter indicating that bishops should send a personal letter to each serviceman every month, along with a copy of the Church magazine at that time, the *Improvement Era*, and a subscription to the *Church News*. That took a little doing. In our large ward, we had about eighteen servicemen. We did not have much money. The priesthood quorums, with effort, supplied funds for the subscriptions to the publications, and

keep the letters coming

I took care of the letter writing. From my experience in the navy at the end of a previous war, I knew the importance of receiving communication from home.

One day the sister who took the shorthand for those individually dictated letters said to me, "Bishop Monson, don't you ever get discouraged?"

I said, "No, I don't. Why?"

"Do you realize," she explained, "that this is the seventeenth consecutive monthly letter you have sent to Lawrence Bryson, and you have never received a reply?"

I said, "Well, send number seventeen. It might do the job." And it did. I received a reply from an APO number in San Francisco. Brother Bryson, far away in the Pacific, had written a short letter, which began, "Dear Bishop, I've been owing you this letter for some time now. But even as I write it, I don't know what I'll talk about, or say. This is the first time I have ever written or tried writing to a bishop.

"How are you and your family? How is the church? How was Christmas? I sure would have liked to be there. It's quite a change from Christmas at home and Christmas here.

"Well, Bishop, I've run out of words already. As you can see I'm still the same backward kid you knew. But I owed you this letter and here it is. Keep the letters coming; it's a pleasure to get them. Tell everyone hello. I'll try to drop you a few lines once in a while. Till then, I'm sincerely yours, Lawrence Bryson.

"P.S. I forgot to thank you for the Church News and magazines. They're great."

I still have that wonderful letter written to me from Lawrence Bryson and dated "Christmas Day, December 25, 1953." It was one of the most treasured Christmas gifts I ever received. Yes, you sometimes wonder after seventeen letters have been sent why no reply has come, but I remembered a line of truth: "The wisdom of God may appear as foolishness to men. But the greatest single lesson we can learn in mortality is that when God speaks and a man obeys, that man will always be right." The leaders of the Church had spoken and had asked us to write to our servicemen. We as bishops needed only to obey. The blessing was sure to follow, and it did.

Some years after this experience, while attending the Salt Lake Cottonwood Stake when James E. Faust served as its president, I related this same account in an effort to encourage attention to our servicemen. After the meeting, a fine-looking young man came forward. He took my hand in his and asked, "Bishop Monson, do you remember me?"

I suddenly realized who he was. "Brother Bryson!" I exclaimed. "How are you? What are you doing in the Church?"

With warmth and obvious pride, he responded, "I'm fine. I serve in the presidency of my elders quorum. Thank you again for your concern for me and the personal letters which you sent and which I treasure."

I do not know
how I can go on

IN ABOUT MARCH 1946, less than a year after the end of World War II, Elder Ezra Taft Benson, then a member of the Quorum of the Twelve, accompanied by Frederick W. Babbel, was assigned a special postwar tour of Europe for the express purpose of meeting with the Saints, assessing their needs, and providing assistance to them. Elder Benson and Brother Babbel later recounted, from a testimony they heard, the experience of a Church member who found herself in an area no longer controlled by the government under which she had resided.

She and her husband had lived an idyllic life in East Prussia. Then had come the second great world war within their lifetimes. Her beloved young husband was killed during the final days of the dreadful fighting in their homeland, leaving her alone to care for their four children.

The occupying forces determined that the Germans in East Prussia must leave their homes and relocate to Western Germany. The woman was German, and so it was necessary for her to go. The journey was over a thousand miles, and she had no way to accomplish it but on foot. She had only a small wagon with wooden wheels in which to convey the family's few possessions. Besides her children and these meager necessities, she took with her a strong faith in God and in the gospel as revealed to the latter-day prophet Joseph Smith.

She and the children began the journey in late summer, gathering what little food they could from the surrounding fields and woods. Millions of refugees and plundering troops were an unrelenting threat.

As the days turned into weeks and the weeks to months, the temperatures dropped below freezing. Each day, she stumbled over the frozen ground, her smallest child—a baby—in her arms. Her three other children struggled along behind her, with the oldest—seven years old—pulling the tiny wooden wagon containing their belongings. Ragged and torn burlap was wrapped around their feet, providing the only protection for them, since their shoes had long since disintegrated. Their thin, tattered jackets covered their thin, tattered clothing, providing their only protection against the cold.

Soon the snows came, and the days and nights became a nightmare. In the evenings she and the children would try to find some kind of shelter—a barn or a shed—and would huddle together for warmth, with a few thin blankets from the wagon on top of them.

She constantly struggled to force from her mind overwhelming fears that they would perish before reaching their destination.

And then one morning the unthinkable happened. As she awakened, she felt a chill in her heart. The tiny form of her three-year-old daughter was cold and still, and she realized that death had claimed the child. Though overwhelmed with grief, she knew that she must take the other children and travel on. First, however, she used the only implement she had—a tablespoon—to dig a grave in the frozen ground for her tiny, precious child.

Death was to be her companion again and again on the journey. Her seven-year-old son died, and again her only shovel was the tablespoon; again she dug hour after hour to lay his mortal remains gently into the earth. The sad task was repeated when her five-year-old son died next.

Her despair was all consuming. She had only her tiny baby daughter left, and the poor thing was failing. When the baby died in her arms, it was almost too much. The spoon was gone now, so hour after hour she dug a grave in the frozen earth with only her frozen fingers. Her grief welled up as she knelt beside the little grave, considering all she had lost.

She wondered, Was it worth going on? How could she bear it, with her heart literally broken? Others were choosing to end their lives rather than continue in such despair.

As she considered the awful possibilities for ending her own life, something within her said, "Get down on your knees and pray." She ignored the prompting until she could resist it no longer. She knelt and prayed more fervently than she had in her entire life:

"Dear Heavenly Father, I do not know how I can go on. I have nothing left except my faith in Thee. I feel, Father, amidst the desolation of my soul, an overwhelming gratitude for the atoning sacrifice of Thy Son, Jesus Christ. I cannot express adequately my love for Him. I know that because He suffered and died, I shall live again with my family; that because He broke the chains of death, I shall see my children again and will have the joy of raising them. Though I do not at this moment wish to live, I will do so, that we may be reunited as a family and return—together—to Thee."

When she finally reached her destination of Karlsruhe, Germany, she was in the throes of starvation. But in a Church meeting shortly thereafter, she bore witness of her happiness and her sure testimony of the Resurrection of Jesus Christ. She had no doubt that, if she remained true to the gospel, she would be reunited with her loved ones in the celestial kingdom of God.

OCCASIONALLY I ponder an experience from my boyhood. I grew up during the Depression. These were difficult times. My father was a craftsman, a printer, and he always had employment, although others were not so fortunate.

the best
Thanksgiving ever

I remember the boys with whom I went to school. Many had clothing bought at rummage sales. The same size jacket was to fit four boys in one family. The father did not support the family. The mother worked nights as a telephone operator in Salt Lake City. The thing I remember most about this family was that when I would call upon the boys to go to school, they would be having breakfast— cornflakes with water. There was no milk, there was no cream, there was no sugar—only cornflakes and water.

One particular Thanksgiving Day there was, as usual, turkey dinner for our family, along with all the trimmings. As I waited for the feast to begin, I heard my name being called by one of my friends, Charlie. In those days we never knocked on the door; we would just stand outside in the back and yell. I heard Charlie call, "Tommy!" I went outside, and he said, "It sure smells good in there. What are you eating?"

I said, "We're eating turkey."

He said, "I've never eaten turkey. What does it taste like?"

I said, "Oh, something like chicken."

"I've never eaten chicken," he said. "What does that taste like?"

I told him to wait a minute, and I went in the house and got a piece of turkey for him to sample. He chewed it for a minute and then said, "Boy, that's good."

I said, "Charlie, what are you having for your Thanksgiving dinner?"

There was a silence, and then he said, "Nothing."

I remembered at that moment my mother, who always fed the transients who came through, riding the rails from east to west. When Mother would welcome them, she'd open the back door and have them sit at the table. Then she'd make them boiled ham sandwiches, give them potato chips and glasses of milk, and ask them what they were doing riding the rails and why they didn't go home and settle down somewhere. She was quite a philosopher and had absolutely no fear whatsoever. I thought of her when my friend Charlie said he was not having Thanksgiving dinner.

At that moment I remembered I had something. I had no money, but I had two white rabbits. They were the pride of my life, beautiful New Zealand whites. I said, "Charlie, you come with me, because I've got something for your Thanksgiving dinner." We went into the backyard, and with tears in my eyes I opened the rabbit hutch, took a gunnysack, and put first one rabbit and then the other into the gunnysack. I said, "You take these home, and your mother will know what to do with them. They taste a whole lot like chicken."

Charlie was up on the fence and over the backyard to his home as quick as a flash. He later said they had the best Thanksgiving dinner they had ever had.

I loved the rabbits, but the feeling that came into my heart on that occasion, when I had given all that I had, when I had followed the counsel and the training of my mother, was superior to any love for those rabbits. I thought of the poet's expression: "The smile of God's approval is the greatest of all gifts."

SOME YEARS AGO I listened intently as a man well beyond middle age told me of an experience in his family history. The widowed mother who had given birth to him and his brothers and sisters had gone to her eternal and well-earned reward. The family assembled at the home and surrounded the large dining-room table. The small metal box in which Mother had kept her earthly treasures was opened reverently. One by one each keepsake was brought forth. There was the wedding certificate from the Salt Lake Temple. "Oh, now Mother can be with Dad," they said. Then there was the deed to the humble home where each child had in turn entered upon the stage of life. The appraised value of the house had little resemblance to the worth Mother had attached to it.

Then there was discovered a yellowed envelope which bore the marks of time. Carefully the flap was opened and from inside was taken a homemade valentine. Its simple message, in the handwriting of a child, read, "I love you, Mother." Though she was gone, by what she held sacred, their mother taught yet another lesson. A silence permeated the room, and every member of the family made a pledge not only to remember, but also to honor mother. 🌿

warning devices

MEN HAVE INVENTED certain safeguards to warn us against danger. When I served in the navy, sonar was in its infant stages. Those of you who have been in the service know that sonar is the device whereby we are warned of an impending vehicle or ship or other obstacle. It has a beep, and the operator becomes accustomed to listening for that beep. When it becomes other than the normal pattern, he knows that danger is at hand, and he can warn the captain and the course can be changed.

When I went to school, many young men had white sidewall tires on their automobiles. These automobiles were equipped with what we called "whiskers"—a little metal device that was attached to the fender of the car. As the car would pull in against the curb, those whiskers would hit the curb, rather than the curb scraping the white sidewall tires, and they would warn that the driver could not go any closer to the curb without damaging his tires.

If man can invent sonar to warn against disaster, and if he can invent whiskers to put on automobile fenders for the protection of white sidewall tires, doesn't it sound reasonable that the Lord would place a warning device within His children to warn us when we are on a detour, away from His pathway? I bear you my testimony that we have a guiding light. It is foolproof if we will but use it. It is known, as you know and as I know, as the Holy Ghost—the still small voice. 🌿

I ONCE HEARD the testimony of Harold Wright, former president of the Mesa Arizona Temple. He related the account of waiting in the temple for the arrival of a busload of Saints from Guatemala City. At that time there was no temple in Guatemala, nor one in Mexico, so the Saints had to come all the way to Arizona. They were a full day and a full evening late, and some of the temple workers began to say, "Well, perhaps they are not coming."

President Wright went into his office and knelt in prayer. As he prayed, a feeling of love came over him for those poverty-stricken Saints from Guatemala. He said, "I knew for a certainty they were coming, and I knew for a certainty they were coming that night. I got up from my knees and went to work. I called together our temple workers and said, 'The Saints from Guatemala will be here shortly. Let us open the cafeteria and prepare a meal for them. They will be hungry. And let us immediately make room in our homes for them. They will need places to stay. They have no money.'"

The next two hours were a flurry of activity in Mesa, Arizona. Then President Wright walked out to the gates of the temple, went down the little pathway to the road, looked at his watch, and said, "They will be here soon." Almost immediately, a little rickety bus came along the road. It was a miracle that the bus ran. It was an even greater miracle that it had come all the way from Guatemala, through Mexico, and up to Arizona. The bus had been

75

so overloaded that the children needed to be passed around from lap to lap in order for everyone to have a seat.

The leader of the group disembarked from the bus and was embraced by the temple president. The brother wept and said, "The Lord has brought us to His house."

President Wright said, "That He has. You must be hungry."

The brother said, "We are not hungry, but our children are." They had all been three days without food. The bus had broken down, and their meager funds had been expended to repair it. They had no money left for food or lodging.

Harold Wright stood only about five feet five or six—but he stood tall before the Lord that night. He said to the leader of the group, "The Lord told us you were coming. We have everything ready for you. Come in and refresh yourselves. We have a beautiful banquet prepared for you, and you will stay in our homes."

President Wright said that the arrival of those Guatemalan Saints was the greatest event in the history of his administration at the Arizona Temple. He said, "We learned something about prayer and revelation. We learned something about love. We learned something about God and His Son, Jesus Christ, and we learned something about ourselves. We truly learned that when we are in the service of our fellow beings, we are only in the service of our God."

IN THE MISSION over which I presided there was a small branch that consisted of two families. I had been invited to be the speaker at one of the meetings. I was not accustomed to such small branches; the ward over which I had presided had 1,050 people. That Sunday we went into the place where the Saints met. It was a rented hall. We didn't meet on the main floor; we met in a room in the basement. There were about nine people present.

this is the day
we begin to build

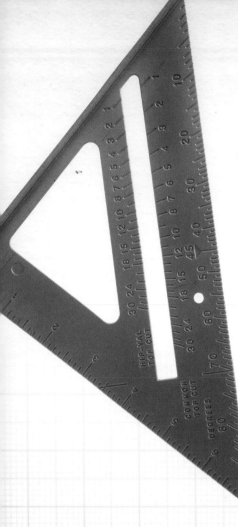

After the meeting, the branch president asked if he could visit with me. He said, "We would like to have a chapel in our branch." Then he opened a copy of one of the Church magazines and showed me pictures of chapels in Australia and New Zealand. He said, "This is the one we would like to build," and he pointed to a building that would house maybe four hundred people and that would cost far more money than they had.

I said, "Oh, you will not be able to afford that until you have several hundred members."

He said, "We intend to have hundreds of members." And then he asked me if I would send six missionaries into his branch. He indicated that his family would personally share the gospel with the city. And this he did.

When the missionaries arrived, he met with them in a store he owned. He said, "Elders, let's pray." And they got down upon their knees and prayed. This branch president then said, "This is the greatest day in the city of St. Thomas. This is the day when the gospel will really begin to be preached with effectiveness in this city. This is the day when we begin to build our new chapel."

The missionaries asked, "Who are we going to teach? We have no investigators." The branch president said, "Hand me the telephone directory." And he turned to the back of the directory where men of all professions were listed. He said, "If we are going to build a new chapel, we need an architect who is a Mormon. And since we don't have an architect who is a member of the Church, we must convert one." Then he went down the list and said, "Who shall be the first Mormon architect in St. Thomas?" And he identified a name. Then he continued with a contractor, and a plumber and an electrician and a doctor and a lawyer. Then he personally went to each and invited him into his house, that the missionaries might present their message and that he and his family could bear their testimonies after the missionaries had given their message.

What was the result of that sharing? I am God's witness that in the three years that I served in eastern Canada, I saw that branch grow from two families to almost three hundred members. They constructed their beautiful chapel. I attended a meeting there with perhaps four hundred persons. What was the secret? It was the attitude "we can achieve our goal." 🌿

SOME YEARS AGO, in the city of Rome, Sister Monson and I met with almost five hundred members of the Church. We noted that the presiding officer at that time was Leopoldo Larcher, a wonderful Italian. His brother had been a guest worker many years before in the auto plants in Germany, where two missionaries had taught him the gospel. Leopoldo's brother went back to Italy and taught the gospel to Leopoldo. He accepted, was baptized, and eventually held many leadership positions in the Church. He was called to be president of the Italy Rome Mission and then president of the Italy Catania Mission. During the meeting in Rome that Sister Monson and I attended, I noticed in that throng of five hundred that there were many in attendance wearing white carnations. I said to Brother Larcher, "What is the significance of the white carnation?"

He said, "Those are new members. We provide a white carnation to every member who has been baptized since our last district conference. Then all the members and all the missionaries know that these people are especially to be fellowshipped."

I watched those Italian members with the white carnations being greeted, embraced, spoken to. They were "no more strangers and foreigners, but fellowcitizens with the saints, and of the household of God" (Ephesians 2:19).

no more strangers

the work of the Lord

OLD BOB was a widower in his eighties when the house in which he was living was to be demolished. I was just a boy when I heard him tell my grandfather his plight as the three of us sat on Grandfather's old front porch swing. With a plaintive voice, he said to Grandfather, "Mr. Condie, I don't know what to do. I have no family. I have no place to go. I have no money." I wondered how Grandfather would answer. Slowly Grandfather reached into his pocket and took from it that old leather purse from which, in response to my hounding, he had produced many a penny or nickel for a special treat. This time he removed a key and handed it to Old Bob. Tenderly he said, "Bob, here is the key to that house I own next door. Take it. Move your things in there and stay as long as you like. There will be no rent to pay and nobody will ever put you out again."

Tears welled up in the eyes of Old Bob, coursed down his cheeks, then disappeared in his long, white beard. Grandfather's eyes were also moist. I spoke no word, but that day my grandfather stood ten feet tall. I was proud to bear his given name. Though I was but a boy, that day I learned a great lesson on reaching outward.

My mother taught me additional lessons on serving others. One common example occurred at dinnertime on Sundays. Just as we children hovered at our so-called starvation level and sat anxiously at the table with the aroma of roast beef filling the room, Mother would say to me, "Tommy, before we eat, take this plate of food I've prepared down the street to Old Bob, and then hurry back."

I could never understand why we couldn't first eat and later deliver his plate of food. I never questioned aloud but would run down to his house and then wait anxiously as Bob's aged feet brought him eventually to the door. Then I would hand him the plate of food. He would present to me the clean plate from the previous Sunday and offer me a dime as pay for my services. My answer was always the same: "I can't accept the money. My mother would tan my hide." He would then run his wrinkled hand through my blond hair and say, "My boy, you have a wonderful mother. Tell her thank you."

You know, I think I never did tell her. I sort of felt Mother didn't need to be told. She seemed to sense his gratitude. I remember, too, that Sunday dinner always seemed to taste a bit better after I had returned from my errand.

When we reach out to others, we participate in the work of the Lord. This is a principle I have experienced again and again throughout my life. I am grateful it was instilled in me at an early age by parents and grandparents who cared.

I REMEMBER WELL the conversion of one family that had been seeking truth. The missionaries called and presented the teachings of the gospel. They studied. They loved what they learned. They were approaching the decision to be baptized.

a message directed to him

One Sunday morning the family, by previous appointment, were preparing to attend the "Mormon" Sunday School. Mother and the children readied themselves but were disappointed when Dad concluded not to attend. They even argued somewhat about the decision. Then Mother and the children went to Sunday School, and Dad angrily stayed at home.

He first attempted to forget the misunderstanding by reading the newspaper, but to no avail. Then he went to his daughter's room and turned on the radio that occupied her nightstand, hoping to hear the news. He didn't hear the news. Rather, he heard the Tabernacle Choir. The message of *Music and the Spoken Word* that day, it seemed, was directed personally to him: "Let not the sun go down upon your wrath" (Ephesians 4:26). This good brother realized the futility of his anger. He was now overpowered by a feeling of gratitude for the message he had just received. When his wife and family returned home, they found him pleasant and happy. His children asked how this change came about. He told them how he had turned to the radio, hoping to get the news, only to be humbled by the message of the Choir in word and song. His daughter said, "Which radio did you use, Dad?"

He answered, "The one on your nightstand."

She replied, "That radio is broken. It hasn't played for weeks."

He led them to the room to prove that this radio did indeed

function. Hadn't he just heard the Choir and a message that had inspired and humbled him? He turned the proper dial. But that radio didn't play. Yet when an honest seeker after truth needed the help of God, that radio did play. The message which led to conversion was received. Needless to say, the family became stalwart members of the Church. 🌿

SOME YEARS AGO, President Hugh B. Brown and I were on a trip to Polynesia. We approached Pago Pago, American Samoa. As we landed, the lovely Samoan children and their leaders came out to meet us. It was very early in the morning—about seven o'clock—and they said, "We need your faith; we have no water. We have been fasting that with you would come moisture from heaven. If we don't have water to-day we will have to close the Mapusaga School, because we are totally dependent upon rainfall for our water supply." It was apparent the lovely Samoan children felt that their fasting would bring forth the blessings of heaven.

As we met in the chapel, President Brown said, "We'd better remember those children." And we offered a prayer. We asked our Heavenly Father to acknowledge their fasting. As President Brown began to speak, we heard the clap of thunder and the sky became dark. Then the rain descended. It descended so loudly against the metal roof that those assembled couldn't hear President Brown. He, with a smile, turned around to me and said, "Tom, now that we've got it turned on, how do we turn it off?" It rained for two hours that morning and the Saints rejoiced. They knew that their fasting had brought forth heaven's blessings. ❧

HE WHOM WE CALL our Heavenly Father will not leave our sincere petition unanswered. This lesson I learned anew some years ago as I received a rather unique and frightening assignment. An acquaintance came to my office one day, having learned that I was about to depart for a lengthy assignment to New Zealand. He told me of his widowed sister, Belva Jones, who had been stricken with terminal cancer, who knew not how to tell her only son—a missionary in that faraway country.

I will see her again

Her wish, even her plea, was that he remain in the mission field and serve faithfully. She worried about his reaction, for the missionary, Elder Ryan Jones, had lost his father just a year earlier to the same dread disease.

I accepted the responsibility. Following a missionary meeting held adjacent to the majestically beautiful New Zealand Temple, I met privately with Elder Jones and, as gently as I could, explained the situation of his mother. Naturally there were tears—not all his—but then the handclasp of assurance and the pledge: "Tell my mother I will serve, I will pray, and I will see her again."

I returned to Salt Lake City just in time to leave once again to attend a conference of the Lost River Stake at Moore, Idaho. As I sat on the stand with the stake president, my attention was drawn almost instinctively to the east side of the chapel, where the morning sunlight bathed the lone occupant of a front bench. I said to the stake president, "Who is the sister upon whom the sunlight is resting? I feel I must speak to her today." He replied, "Her name is Belva Jones. She has a missionary son in New Zealand. She is very ill and has requested a blessing."

Prior to that moment, I had not known where Belva Jones lived. My assignment that weekend could have been to any one of fifty stakes. Yet the Lord, in His own way, had answered the prayer of faith of a concerned mother. We had a wonderful visit together. I reported word for word the reaction and the resolve of her son, Ryan. A blessing was provided, a prayer offered, a witness received. Belva Jones would live to see her son complete his mission. Just one month prior to her passing, his mission completed, Ryan returned home. 🌿

LONG YEARS AGO Roy Kohler and
Grant Remund served together in Church capaci-
ties. They were the best of friends. They were tillers
of the soil and dairymen. Then a misunderstanding
arose that created somewhat of a rift between them.

if ye have love

Later, when Roy Kohler became grievously ill with cancer and had but a limited time to live, my wife, Frances, and I visited Roy and I gave him a blessing. As we talked afterward, Brother Kohler said, "Let me tell you about one of the sweetest experiences I have had during my life." He then recounted to me his misunderstanding with Grant Remund and the ensuing estrangement. "We were on the outs with each other," he commented.

"Then," continued Roy, "I had just put up our hay for the winter to come, when one night, as a result of spontaneous combustion, the hay caught fire, burning the hay, the barn, and everything in it right to the ground. I was devastated," said Roy. "I didn't know what in the world I would do. The night was dark, except for the dying embers of the fire. Then I saw coming toward me from the road, in the direction of Grant Remund's place, the lights of tractors and heavy equipment. As the 'rescue party' turned in our drive and met me amidst my tears, Grant said, 'Roy, you've got quite a mess to clean up. My boys and I are here. Let's get to it.'" Together they plunged to the task at hand. Gone forever was the wedge that had separated them for a short time. They worked throughout the night and into the next day, with many others in the community joining in.

May we ever be exemplary in our homes and faithful in keeping all of the commandments, that we may harbor no destructive grudges but rather remember the Savior's admonition: "By this shall all men know that ye are my disciples, if ye have love one to another" (John 13:35).

stranded in the snow

THE OPPORTUNITY to be a blessing in the life of another often comes unexpectedly. On one extremely cold Saturday night one winter, Sister Monson and I drove several miles to the mountain valley of Midway, Utah, where we have a home. The temperature that night was minus 24 degrees Fahrenheit, and we wanted to make certain all was well at our home there. We checked and found that it was fine, so we left to return to Salt Lake City. We barely made it the few miles to the highway before our car stopped working. We were completely stranded. I have seldom, if ever, been as cold as we were that night.

Reluctantly we began walking toward the nearest town, the cars whizzing past us. Finally one car stopped, and a young man offered to help. We eventually found that the diesel fuel in our gas tank had thickened because of the cold, making it impossible for us to drive the car. This kind young man drove us back to our Midway home. I attempted to reimburse him for his services, but he graciously declined. He indicated that he was a Boy Scout and wanted to do a good turn. I identified myself to him, and he expressed his appreciation for the privilege to be of help. Assuming that he was about missionary age, I asked him if he had plans to serve a mission. He indicated he was not certain just what he wanted to do.

On the following Monday morning, I wrote a letter to this young man and thanked him for his kindness. In the letter I encouraged him to serve a full-time mission. I enclosed a copy of one of my books and underscored the chapters on missionary service.

About a week later the young man's mother telephoned and advised that her son was an outstanding young man but that because of certain influences in his life, his long-held desire to serve a mission had diminished. She indicated that she and his father had fasted and prayed that his heart would be changed. They had placed his name on the prayer roll of the Provo Utah Temple. They hoped that somehow, in some way, his heart would be touched for good and he would return to his desire to fill a mission and to serve the Lord faithfully. The mother wanted me to know that she looked upon the events of that cold evening as an answer to their prayers in his behalf. I said, "I agree with you."

After several months and more communication with this young man, Sister Monson and I were overjoyed to attend his missionary farewell prior to his departure for the Canada Vancouver Mission.

Was it chance that our paths crossed on that cold December night? I do not for one moment believe so. Rather, I believe our meeting was an answer to a mother's and father's heartfelt prayers for the son they cherished.

Our Heavenly Father is aware of our needs and will help us as we call upon Him for assistance. I believe that no concern of ours is too small or insignificant. The Lord is in the details of our lives.

MANY YEARS AGO there was a young woman, Baur Dee Sheffield, who taught in Mutual. She had no children of her own, though she and her husband dearly longed for children. Her love was expressed through devotion to her special young women as each week she taught them eternal truths and lessons of life. Then came illness, followed by death. She was but twenty-seven.

to Baur Dee,
from your girls

Each year, on Memorial Day, her Mutual girls made a pilgrimage to the graveside of their teacher, always leaving flowers and a card signed, "To Baur Dee, from your girls." First there were ten girls who went, then five, then two, and eventually just one, who continued to visit each Memorial Day, always placing on the grave a bouquet of flowers and a card, inscribed as always, "To Baur Dee, from your girls."

One year, nearly twenty-five years after Baur Dee's death, the only one of "her girls" who continued to visit the grave realized she would be away on Memorial Day and decided to visit her teacher's grave a few days early. She had gathered flowers, tied them with a ribbon, attached a card, and was putting on her jacket to leave when her doorbell rang. She opened the door and was greeted by one of her visiting teachers, Colleen Fuller, who said she had experienced difficulty getting together with her visiting teaching partner and so had decided to come alone and unannounced in an effort to complete her visiting teaching before the end of the month. As Colleen was invited in, she noticed the jacket and flowers and apologized for obviously interrupting whatever had been planned.

"No problem," came the response. "I'm just on my way to the cemetery to put flowers on the grave of the woman who was my Mutual teacher, who had a profound influence on me and the other girls she taught. Originally about ten of us visited her grave each year to express our love and thanks to her, but now I represent the group."

Colleen asked, "Could your teacher's name have been Baur Dee?"

"Why, yes," came the answer. "How did you know?"

With a catch in her voice, Colleen said, "Baur Dee was my aunt—my mother's sister. Every Memorial Day since she died, my family has found on her grave a bouquet of flowers and a card inscribed from Baur Dee's girls. They've always wanted to know who these girls were so they could thank them for remembering Baur Dee. Now I can let them know."

participating

in a miracle

IN FARAWAY BUCHAREST, Romania, Lynn Oborn, a physical therapist volunteering at an orphanage, was attempting to teach little Raymond, who had never walked, how to use his legs. Raymond had been born with severe club feet and was completely blind. Recent orthopedic surgery had corrected the club feet, but Raymond was still unable to use his legs. Lynn Oborn knew that a child-size walker would enable Raymond to get on his feet, but such a walker was not available anywhere in Romania. I'm sure fervent prayers were offered by this doctor who had done all he could without a walking aid for the boy. Blindness can hamper a child, but inability to walk, to run, to play can injure his precious spirit.

Let us turn now to Provo, Utah. The Richard Headlee family, learning of the suffering and pitiful conditions in Romania, joined with others to assemble a forty-foot container filled with forty thousand pounds of needed supplies, including food, clothing, medicine, blankets, and toys. The project deadline arrived, and the container had to be shipped that day. No one involved with the project knew of the particular need for a child-size walker. However, at the last possible moment, a family brought forth a child's walker and placed it in the container.

When the anxiously awaited container arrived at the orphanage in Bucharest, Lynn Oborn was present as it was opened. Every item it contained would be put to immediate use at the orphanage. As the Headlee family introduced themselves to Lynn Oborn, he said, "Oh, I hope you brought me a child's walker for Raymond!"

One of the Headlee family members responded, "I can vaguely remember something like a walker, but I don't know its size." Another family member was dispatched back into the container, crawling among all the bales of clothes and boxes of food, searching for the walker. When he found it, he lifted it up and cried out, "It's a little one!" Cheers erupted—which quickly turned to tears, for they all knew they had been part of a modern-day miracle. There may be some who say, "We don't have miracles today." But the physical therapist whose prayers were answered would respond, "Oh, yes we do, and Raymond is walking!"

I LEARNED TO SWIM in the swift-running currents of the Provo River in beautiful Provo Canyon. The "old swimming hole" was in a deep portion of the river, formed by a large rock that had fallen into the river, I assume, when the workmen constructing the railroad were blasting through the canyon. The pool was dangerous, what with its depth of sixteen feet, its current moving swiftly against the large rock, and the sucking action of the whirlpools below the rock. It was not a place for a novice or inexperienced swimmer.

save her! save her!

One warm summer afternoon when I was about twelve or thirteen, I took a large, inflated inner tube from a tractor tire, slung it over my shoulder, and walked barefoot up the railroad track that followed the course of the river. I entered the water about a mile above the swimming hole, sat comfortably in the tube, and enjoyed a leisurely float down the river. The river held no fear for me, for I knew its secrets.

That day the Greek-speaking people in Utah held a reunion at Vivian Park in Provo Canyon, as they did every year. Native food, games, and dances were the order of the day. But some left the party to try swimming in the river. When they arrived at the swimming hole, it was deserted, for afternoon shadows were beginning to envelop it.

As my inflated tube bobbed up and down, I was about to enter the swiftest portion of the river just at the head of the swimming hole when I heard frantic cries, "Save her! Save her!" A young lady swimmer, accustomed to the still waters of a gymnasium swimming pool, had fallen from the rock into the treacherous whirlpools. None of the party could swim to save her. Suddenly I appeared on the potentially tragic scene. I saw the top of her head disappearing under the water for the third time, there to descend to a watery grave. I stretched forth my hand, grasped her hair, and lifted her over the side of the tube and into my arms. At the pool's lower end, the water was slower as I paddled the tube, with my precious cargo, to her waiting relatives and friends. They threw their arms around the water-soaked girl and kissed her, crying, "Thank God! Thank God you are safe!" Then they hugged and kissed me. I was embarrassed and quickly returned to the tube and continued my float down to the Vivian Park bridge. The water was frigid, but I was not cold, for I was filled with a warm feeling. I realized that I had participated in the saving of a life. Heavenly Father had heard the cries, "Save her! Save her," and permitted me, a deacon, to float by at precisely the time I was needed.

That day I learned that the sweetest feeling in mortality is to realize that God, our Heavenly Father, knows each one of us and generously permits us to see and to share His divine power to save.

people can change

MANY YEARS AGO, before I left to become president of the Canadian Mission, I developed a friendship with a man by the name of Shelley, who lived in my ward area but who did not embrace the gospel, despite the fact that his wife and children had become members of the Church. He had been known as the toughest man in town when he was young. Try as I might, I could not bring about a change in Shelley's attitude toward the Church. He was unalterably opposed to it. The task appeared hopeless. In time Shelley and his family moved from our ward.

After I had returned from Canada and was called to the Twelve, I received a telephone call from Shelley. He said, "Will you seal my wife and me and our family in the Salt Lake Temple?"

I answered hesitatingly, "But Shelley, you first must be a baptized member of the Church."

He laughed and responded, "Oh, I took care of that while you were in Canada. My home teacher was a school crossing guard, and every weekday, as he and I would visit at the crossing, we would discuss the gospel."

Had someone asked me, before we left for Canada, who of all my acquaintances I would consider the least likely candidate for baptism, I would probably have given Shelley's name. Yes, people can change. 🌿

a very special pigeon

AS A BOY of fifteen I was called to preside over a quorum of teachers. Our adviser was interested in us, and we knew it. One day he said to me, "Tom, you enjoy raising pigeons, don't you?"

I responded with a warm "Yes."

Then he proffered, "How would you like me to give you a pair of purebred Birmingham Roller pigeons?"

This time I answered, "Yes, sir!" You see, the pigeons I had were just the common variety trapped on the roof of the Grant Elementary School.

He invited me to come to his home the next evening. The next day was one of the longest in my young life. I was awaiting my adviser's return from work an hour before he arrived. He took me to his loft, which was in a small barn at the rear of his yard. As I looked at the most beautiful pigeons I had yet seen, he said, "Select any male, and I will give you a female which is different from any other pigeon in the world." I made my selection. He then placed in my hand a tiny hen. I asked what made her so different. He responded, "Look carefully, and you'll notice that she has but one eye." Sure enough, one eye was missing, a cat having done the damage. "Take them home to your loft," he counseled. "Keep them in for about ten days and then turn them out to see if they will remain at your place."

I followed his instructions. When I released them, the male pigeon strutted about the roof of the loft, then returned inside to eat.

But the one-eyed female was gone in an instant. I called Harold, my adviser, and asked, "Did that one-eyed pigeon return to your loft?"

"Come on over," said he, "and we'll have a look."

As we walked from his kitchen door to the loft, my adviser commented, "Tom, you are the president of the teachers quorum." This I already knew. Then he added, "What are you going to do to activate Bob?"

I answered, "I'll have him at quorum meeting this week."

Then he reached up to a special nest and handed to me the one-eyed pigeon. "Keep her in for a few days and try again." This I did, and once more she disappeared. Again the experience, "Come on over and we'll see if she returned here." Came the comment as we walked to the loft, "Congratulations on getting Bob to priesthood meeting. Now what are you and Bob going to do to activate Bill?"

"We'll have him there this week," I volunteered.

This experience was repeated over and over again. I was a grown man before I fully realized that, indeed, Harold, my adviser, had given me a special pigeon, the only bird in his loft he knew would return every time she was released. It was his inspired way of having an ideal personal priesthood interview with the teachers quorum president every two weeks. I owe a lot to that one-eyed pigeon. I owe more to that quorum adviser. He had the patience to help me prepare for opportunities that lay ahead. 🌿

I know this work is true

Not long after his arrival, together with his companion he called at the home of Elmer Pollard in Oshawa, Ontario, Canada. Feeling sorry for the young men, who were going house to house, Mr. Pollard invited the missionaries into his home. They presented to him their message. He did not catch the Spirit. In due time he asked that they leave and not return. His last words to the elders as they departed his front porch were spoken in derision: "You can't tell me you actually believe Joseph Smith was a prophet of God!"

The door was shut. The elders walked down the path. Our country boy spoke to his companion: "Elder, we didn't respond to Mr. Pollard. He said we didn't believe Joseph Smith was a true prophet. Let's return and bear our testimonies to him." At first the more experienced missionary hesitated, but finally he agreed to accompany his companion. Fear struck their hearts as they approached the door from which they had just been ejected. They knocked, confronted Mr. Pollard, spent an agonizing moment, and then with power borne of the Spirit, our inexperienced missionary spoke: "Mr. Pollard, you said we didn't really believe Joseph Smith was a prophet of God. I testify to you that Joseph was a prophet. He did translate the Book of Mormon. He saw God the Father and Jesus the Son. I know it."

Some time later, Mr. Pollard, now Brother Pollard, stood in a priesthood meeting and declared: "That night I could not sleep. Resounding in my ears I heard the words: 'Joseph Smith was a prophet of God. I know it. I know it. I know it.' The next day I telephoned the missionaries and asked them to return. Their message, coupled with their testimonies, changed my life and the lives of my family." 🦋

He knows the end
from the beginning

I SERVED in the United States Navy toward the end of World War II. I was what is called a seaman, the lowest possible rank in the navy. Then I qualified to be seaman first class; then I qualified to be yeoman third class.

The war ended, and I was later discharged. But I made a decision that if ever I went back into the military, I wanted to serve as a commissioned officer. Now, if you haven't been in the military, I won't take the time to tell you the difference between the apprentice seaman and the commissioned officer. One can only learn that by experience, but once learned one never forgets. I thought, *no more mess kitchens for me, no more scrubbing of the decks, if I can avoid it,* and I worked like a slave to qualify for that commission.

I'd been discharged. I rejoined the United States Naval Reserve. I went to drill every Monday night at Fort Douglas. I studied hard that I might qualify academically. I took every kind of examination imaginable: mental, physical, and emotional. Finally, there came from Denver, Colorado, the beautiful news, "You have been accepted to receive the commission of an ensign in the United States Naval Reserve." I gleefully showed it to my wife, Frances, and said, "I made it! I made it!" She hugged me and said, "You've worked hard enough to achieve it."

But then something happened. I was called to be a counselor in my ward bishopric. The bishop's council meeting was on the same evening as my navy drill meeting. I knew there was a terrible conflict. I knew that I didn't have the time to pursue the naval reserve and my bishopric duties. What was I to do? A decision had to be made.

I prayed about it. And then I went to see my boyhood stake president, Elder Harold B. Lee. I sat down across the table from him. I told him how much I valued that commission. In fact, I showed him the copy of the letter of appointment I had received. And then he said to me, after pondering: "Here's what you should do, Brother Monson. You write a letter to the Bureau of Naval Affairs and tell them that because of your call as a member of the bishopric, you can't accept that commission in the United States Naval Reserve." My heart sank. Then he said, "Then write to the commandant of the Twelfth Naval District in San Francisco and tell them that you would like to be discharged from the reserve." I don't know how I survived that interview.

I said, "Brother Lee, you don't understand the military. Of course they will decline to give me that commission if I refuse to accept it, but the Twelfth Naval District isn't going to let me off. A noncommissioned officer will surely be called up, with a war brewing in Korea. If they are called back, I would rather go back as a commissioned officer, but I won't if I don't accept this commission. Are you sure this is the counsel you want me to receive?" Those who know Brother Lee know that I was on dangerous ground in questioning him twice. He put his hand on my shoulder and in a fatherly way said, "Brother Monson, have more faith. The military is not for you."

I went to my home. I placed a tear-stained commission back in its envelope with its accompanying letter and declined to accept it. I then wrote a letter to the Twelfth Naval District and requested a discharge from the naval reserve.

My discharge from the naval reserve was in the last group processed before the outbreak of the Korean War. My headquarters outfit was activated. Six weeks after I had been called to be a counselor in the bishopric, I was called to be the bishop of my ward. I would not be standing in the position I now hold had I not followed the counsel of a prophet.

I testify with all the strength and all the fervor of my conviction that our Heavenly Father will guide and bless you in the important decisions that you will be called upon to make. He knows the end from the beginning. If you follow the counsel of His appointed servants, you will be blessed. 🍃

a living testimony
of the gospel

SOME YEARS AGO, while visiting the members and missionaries in Australia, I witnessed a sublime example depicting how a treasury of testimony can bless and sanctify a home. The mission president, Horace D. Ensign, and I were traveling the long distance from Sydney to Darwin, where I was to break ground for our first chapel in that city. En route we had a scheduled stop at a mining community named Mt. Isa. As we entered the small airport at Mt. Isa, a woman and her two children approached. She said, "I am Judith Louden, a member of the Church, and these are my two children. We learned you would be on this flight, so we have come to visit with you during your brief stopover." She explained that her husband was not a member of the Church and that she and the children were indeed the only members in the entire area. We shared lessons and bore testimony.

Time passed. As we prepared to reboard, Sister Louden looked so forlorn, so alone. She pleaded, "You can't go yet; I have so missed the Church." Suddenly the loudspeaker announced a thirty-minute mechanical delay of our flight. Sister Louden whispered, "My prayer has just been answered." She then asked how she might influence her husband to show an interest in the gospel. We counseled her to include him in their home Primary lesson each week and be to him a living testimony of the gospel. I mentioned we would send to her a subscription to *The Children's Friend* and additional helps for her family teaching. We urged that she never give up on her husband.

We departed Mt. Isa, a city to which I have never returned. I shall, however, always hold dear in memory that sweet mother and those precious children extending a tear-filled expression and a fond wave of gratitude and good-bye.

Several years later, while speaking at a priesthood leadership meeting in Brisbane, Australia, I emphasized the significance of gospel scholarship in the home and the importance of living the gospel and being examples of the truth. I shared with the men assembled the account of Sister Louden and the impact her faith and determination had made on me. As I concluded, I said, "I suppose I'll never know if Sister Louden's husband ever joined the Church, but he couldn't have found a better model to follow."

One of the leaders raised his hand, then stood and declared, "Brother Monson, I am Richard Louden. The woman of whom you speak is my wife. The children [his voice quavered] are our children. We are a forever family now, thanks in part to the persistence and the patience of my dear wife. She did it all." Not a word was spoken. The silence was broken only by sniffles and was marked by many tears.

Let us determine, whatever our circumstance, to make of our houses happy homes. Let us open wide the windows of our hearts, that each family member may feel welcome and "at home."

IN THE FRANTIC PACE

of life today, provide place for prayer. Our task is larger than ourselves. We need God's divine help. I testify that His help is but a prayer away.

help is a prayer away

Once, when I had the privilege of attending the annual meetings of the Boy Scouts of America, I took with me several copies of the *New Era* that I might share this excellent publication with officials of Scouting. As I opened the package, I found that my secretary, for no accountable reason, had given me two extra copies of the June issue, an issue that featured temple marriage. I left the two copies in the hotel room and, as planned, distributed the other copies.

On the final day of the conference, I had no desire to attend the scheduled luncheon but felt compelled to return to my room. As I entered, the telephone was ringing. The caller introduced herself as Sister Knotts. She asked if I could provide a blessing for her ten-year-old daughter. I agreed readily, and she indicated that she, her daughter, her son, and her husband would come immediately to my hotel room. As I waited, I prayed for help. The applause of the convention was replaced by the peace of prayer.

Then came the knock at the door and the privilege of meeting a choice Latter-day Saint family. Ten-year-old Deanna walked with the aid of crutches. Cancer had required the amputation of her left leg. Her clothing was clean, her countenance radiant, her trust in God unwavering. A blessing was provided. Mother and son knelt by the side of the bed while the father and I placed our hands on tiny Deanna. We were directed by the Spirit of God. We were humbled by its power. I felt the tears course down my cheeks and tumble upon my hands as they rested on the head of that beautiful child of God. I spoke of eternal ordinances and family exaltation. The Lord prompted me to urge this family to enter the holy temple of

God. At the conclusion of the blessing, I learned that such a temple visit was planned for that very summer. Questions pertaining to the temple were asked. I heard no heavenly voice, nor did I see a vision. Yet there came to me a certain statement: "Refer to the *New Era*." I looked to the dresser, and there were the two copies of the temple issue of the *New Era*. One was given to Deanna. One was provided her parents. Each was reviewed and read.

The Knotts family said farewell, and once again the room was still. A prayer of gratitude came easily. Once more I felt the resolve to provide place for prayer.

WHEN I WAS a new mission president, there sat in my office one day a newly arrived missionary. He was bright, strong, filled with enthusiasm and a desire to serve, happy and grateful to be a missionary. As I spoke with him, I said, "Elder, I imagine that your father and mother wholeheartedly support you in your mission call." He lowered his head and replied, "Well, not quite. You see, President, my father is not a member of the Church. He doesn't believe as we believe, so he cannot fully appreciate the importance of my assignment."

your father will join

Without hesitating, and prompted by a source not my own, I said to him, "Elder, if you will honestly and diligently serve God in proclaiming His message, your father will join the Church before your mission is concluded." He clasped my hand in a viselike grip; the tears welled up in his eyes and began to roll forth down his cheeks, and he declared, "To see my father accept the truth would be the greatest blessing that could come into my life."

This young man did not sit idly by hoping and wishing that the promise would be fulfilled, but rather he followed the example of Abraham Lincoln, of whom it has been said, "When he prayed, he prayed as though everything depended upon God, and then he worked as though everything depended upon him." Such was the missionary service of this young man.

At every missionary conference I would seek him out before the meetings would ever commence and ask, "Elder, how's Dad progressing?"

His reply would invariably be, "No progress, President, but I know the Lord will fulfill the promise given to me through you as my mission president." The days turned to weeks and the weeks to months, and, finally, just two weeks before we ourselves left the mission field to return home, I received a letter from the father of this missionary. In it, he reported that he had been baptized one week before his faithful son returned home from his mission.

The humble prayer of faith had once again been answered. 🌿

ON MY FIRST VISIT to the fabled village of Sauniatu, Samoa, so loved by President David O. McKay, my wife and I met with a large gathering of small children. At the conclusion of our messages to these shy yet beautiful youngsters, I suggested to the native Samoan teacher that we go forward with the closing exercises. As he announced the final hymn, I suddenly felt compelled to personally greet each of these 247 children. My watch revealed that the time was too short for such a privilege, so I discounted the impression. Before the benediction was to be spoken, I again felt this strong impression to shake the hand of each child. This time I made the desire known to the instructor, who displayed a broad and beautiful Samoan smile. He spoke in Samoan to the children, and they beamed their approval of his comments.

The instructor then revealed to me the reason for his and their joy. He said, "When we learned that President McKay had assigned a member of the Quorum of the Twelve to visit us in faraway Samoa, I told the children if they would each one earnestly and sincerely pray and exert faith like the Bible accounts of old, that the Apostle would visit our tiny village at Sauniatu, and through their faith, he would be impressed to greet each child with a personal handclasp." Tears could not be restrained as each of those precious boys and girls walked shyly by and whispered softly to us a sweet *talofa lava*. The gift of faith had been evidenced.

blessed through their faith

the wisdom of
being obedient

THE GREAT TEST of this life is obedience. "We will prove them herewith," said the Lord, "to see if they will do all things whatsoever the Lord their God shall command them" (Abraham 3:25).

We learn obedience throughout our lives. Beginning when we are very young, those responsible for our care set forth guidelines and rules to ensure our safety. Life would be simpler for all of us if we would obey such rules completely. Many of us, however, learn through experience the wisdom of being obedient.

When I was growing up, each summer from early July until early September my family stayed at our cabin at Vivian Park in Provo Canyon in Utah.

One of my best friends during those carefree days in the canyon was Danny Larsen, whose family also owned a cabin at Vivian Park. Each day he and I roamed this boys' paradise, fishing in the stream and the river, collecting rocks and other treasures, hiking, climbing, and simply enjoying each minute of each hour of each day.

One morning Danny and I decided we wanted to have a campfire that evening with all our canyon friends. We just needed to clear an area in a nearby field where we could all gather. The June grass that covered the field had become dry and prickly, making the field unsuitable for our purposes. We began to pull at the tall grass, planning to clear a large, circular area. We tugged and yanked with all our might, but all we could get were small handfuls of the stubborn weeds. We knew this task would take the entire day, and already our energy and enthusiasm were waning.

And then what I thought was the perfect solution came into my eight-year-old mind. I said to Danny, "All we need is to set these weeds on fire. We'll just burn a circle in the weeds!" He readily agreed, and I ran to our cabin to get a few matches.

Lest any of you think that at the tender age of eight we were permitted to use matches, I want to make it clear that both Danny and I were forbidden to use them without adult supervision. Both of us had been warned repeatedly of the dangers of fire. However, I knew where my family kept the matches, and we needed to clear that field. Without so much as a second thought, I ran to our cabin and grabbed a few matchsticks, making certain no one was watching. I hid them quickly in one of my pockets.

Back to Danny I ran, excited that in my pocket I had the solution to our problem. I recall thinking that the fire would burn only as far as we wanted and then would somehow magically extinguish itself.

I struck a match on a rock and set the parched June grass ablaze. It ignited as though it had been drenched in gasoline. At first Danny and I were thrilled as we watched the weeds disappear, but it soon became apparent that the fire was not about to go out on its own. We panicked as we realized there was nothing we could do to stop it. The menacing flames began to follow the wild grass up the mountainside, endangering the pine trees and everything else in their path.

Finally we had no option but to run for help. Soon all available men and women at Vivian Park were dashing back and forth with wet burlap bags, beating at the flames in an attempt to extinguish them. After several hours the last remaining embers were smothered. The ages-old pine trees had been saved, as had the homes the flames would eventually have reached.

Danny and I learned several difficult but important lessons that day—not the least of which was the importance of obedience.

There are rules and laws to help ensure our physical safety. Likewise, the Lord has provided guidelines and commandments to help ensure our spiritual safety so that we might successfully navigate this often-treacherous mortal existence and return eventually to our Heavenly Father. Declared the Savior, "For all who will have a blessing at my hands shall abide the law which was appointed for that blessing, and the conditions thereof, as were instituted from before the foundation of the world" (Doctrine and Covenants 132:5).

The knowledge which we seek, the answers for which we yearn, and the strength which we desire today to meet the challenges of a complex and changing world can be ours when we willingly obey the Lord's commandments.

whom God calls,
God qualifies

MANY YEARS AGO, President Spencer W. Kimball shared with President Gordon B. Hinckley, Elder Bruce R. McConkie, and me an experience he had in the appointment of a patriarch for the Shreveport Louisiana Stake of the Church. President Kimball described how he interviewed, how he searched, and how he prayed that he might learn the Lord's will concerning the selection. For some reason, none of the suggested candidates was the man for this assignment at this particular time.

The day wore on. The evening meetings began. Suddenly President Kimball turned to the stake president and asked him to identify a particular man seated perhaps two-thirds of the way back from the front of the chapel. The stake president replied that the individual was James Womack, whereupon President Kimball said, "He is the man the Lord has selected to be your stake patriarch. Please have him meet with me in the high council room following the meeting."

The stake president, Charles Cagle, was startled, for James Womack did not wear the label of a typical man. He had sustained terrible injuries while in combat during World War II. He lost both hands and one arm, as well as most of his eyesight and part of his hearing. Nobody had wanted to let him into law school when he returned, yet he finished third in his class at Louisiana State University. James Womack simply refused to wear the label "Handicapped."

That evening, as President Kimball met with Brother Womack and informed him that the Lord had designated him to be the patriarch, there was a protracted silence in the room. Then Brother Womack said: "President Kimball, it is my understanding that a patriarch is to place his hands on the head of the person he blesses. As you can see, I have no hands to place on the head of anyone."

President Kimball, in his kind and patient manner, invited Brother Womack to make his way to the back of the chair on which President Kimball was seated. He then said, "Now, Brother Womack, lean forward and see if the stumps of your arms will reach the top of my head." To Brother Womack's joy, they touched President Kimball, and the exclamation came forth, "I can reach you! I can reach you!"

"Of course you can reach me," responded President Kimball. "And if you can reach me, you can reach any whom you bless. I will be the shortest person you will ever have seated before you."

President Kimball reported to us that when the name of James Womack was presented to the stake conference, "the hands of the members shot heavenward in an enthusiastic vote of approval."

Whom God calls, God qualifies. 🌿

IN MY CHILDHOOD, everything wasn't bliss in our ward Primary, for boys will be boys. The laughter of the boys and the chatter of the girls at times must have been most disconcerting to our Primary leaders.

you're my
Primary boy

One day as we left the chapel for our classrooms, I noted that our Primary president remained behind. I paused and observed her. She sat all alone on the front row of the benches, took out her handkerchief, and began to weep. I walked up to her and said, "Sister Georgell, don't cry."

She said, "I'm sad."

I responded, "What's the matter?"

She said, "I can't control the Trail Builders. Will you help me?"

Of course I answered, "Yes."

She said, "Oh, that would be wonderful, Tommy, if you would."

What I didn't know then is that I was the source of her tears. She had effectively enlisted me to aid in achieving reverence in our Primary, and it was achieved.

The years flew by. When Melissa Georgell was in her nineties, she lived in a nursing facility in the northwest part of Salt Lake City. One year just before Christmas, I determined to visit my beloved Primary president. Over the car radio I heard the music of familiar Christmas carols: "Hark! the Herald Angels Sing," "O Little Town of Bethlehem," and many others. I reflected on the visit made by wise men those long years ago and the visit made by us boys when we portrayed the wise men in the pageant. The wise men brought precious gifts to the Christ child. I brought to Melissa only the gift of love and a desire to say "Thank you."

I found her in the lunchroom. She was staring at her plate of food, teasing it with the fork she held in her aged hand. Not a bite did she eat. As I spoke to her, my words were met by a benign but blank stare. I gently took her fork from her and began to feed her, talking all the time I did so about her service to boys and girls as a Primary worker and the joy that was mine to have served later as her bishop. There wasn't even a glimmer of recognition, far less a spoken word. Two other residents of the nursing home gazed at me with puzzled expressions. At last they spoke, saying, "She doesn't know anyone—even her own family. She hasn't said a word for a long, long time."

Luncheon ended. My one-sided conversation wound down. I stood to leave. I held her frail hand in mine and gazed into her wrinkled but beautiful countenance and said, "God bless you, Melissa, and merry Christmas."

Without warning, she spoke the words, "I know you. You're Tommy Monson, my Primary boy. How I love you."

She pressed my hand to her lips and bestowed on it the kiss of love. Tears coursed down her cheeks and bathed our clasped hands. Those hands, that day, were hallowed by heaven and graced by God. The herald angels did sing, for I heard them in my heart. 🦋

ONE WINTER, a twelve-year-old Mongolian boy, Amarah, was tending his family's flock of sheep the night a blizzard hit. Driving snow and biting wind blasted the Mongolian countryside with deadly cold as the young boy fought to stay alive and survive the night. They found him the next day—alive, but so severely frostbitten that local physicians were forced to amputate both of his legs just below the knees.

From then on, he had to be carried wherever he wanted to go. He was forced to drop out of school, and when he reached the age where his friends were finding employment, Amarah remained at home, immobile and feeling useless.

Eventually, he moved in with his sister and her husband, both of whom were members of the Church. He began developing friendships with the missionaries of the local Songino Branch, who would come to visit the family. Five years after the fateful night of the storm, Amarah entered the waters of baptism.

Early on Sunday mornings, the elders arrived at the house and carried Amarah on their backs to church. When the meetings were over, they carried him back to his home.

President Gibbons of the Mongolia Ulaanbaatar Mission learned of Amarah's circumstances and determined to help in some way. He found that Amarah's sister and brother-in-law had been trying to save money so that Amarah could one day obtain a set of prosthetic legs; however, it would be many, many years before they would have enough—if that time ever came. President Gibbons determined to supplement their efforts with fast offerings, and by September of 2002, seven months after Amarah's baptism, everything was in place for an operation that would prepare his legs for the prosthetics. He told the missionaries, "The next time I go to church, I will get there by myself."

The operation was a success, and Amarah was fitted with the prosthetic limbs. Soon, with the help of temporary crutches, he made his way to church. The next week he showed up with only one crutch. And then, the following week, he walked to church with a cane. That day he passed the sacrament for the first time to a teary-eyed branch. 🌿

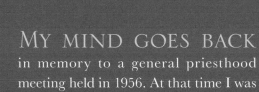

MY MIND GOES BACK in memory to a general priesthood meeting held in 1956. At that time I was serving in the stake presidency of the Temple View Stake in Salt Lake City.

I'll be forever grateful

Percy K. Fetzer, John R. Burt, and I, the stake presidency, had come to the Tabernacle early, that hopefully we might find a place to sit. We were among the first to enter the Tabernacle and had almost two hours to wait before the meeting would begin.

President Fetzer related to President Burt and me an experience from his missionary days in Germany. He described how one rainy night he and his companion were to present a gospel message to a group assembled in a schoolhouse. A protester had broadcast falsehoods concerning the Church, and a number of people threatened violence against the two missionaries. At a critical moment, a woman who was a widow stepped between the elders and the angry group and said, "These young men are my guests and are coming to my home now. Please make way for us to leave." The crowd parted, and the missionaries walked through the rainy night with their benefactress, arriving at length at her modest home. She placed their wet coats over the kitchen chairs and invited the missionaries to sit at the table while she prepared food for them. After eating, the elders presented a message to the kind lady who had befriended them. A young son of the woman was invited to come to the table, but he refused, preferring his position of solitude and warmth directly behind the kitchen stove.

President Fetzer concluded the account with the comment, "While I don't know if that woman ever joined the Church, I'll be forever grateful to her for her kindness that rain-drenched night thirty-three years ago."

The brethren sitting in front of us in the Tabernacle had been speaking to one another also. After a while we began listening to their conversation. One asked the friend sitting next to him, "Tell me how you came to be a member of the Church."

The brother responded, "One rainy night in Germany my mother brought to our house two drenched missionaries whom she had rescued from a mob. Mother fed the elders, and they presented to her a message concerning the work of the Lord. They invited me to join the discussion, but I was shy and fearful, so I remained secure in my seat behind the stove. Later, when I once more heard about the Church, I remembered the courage and faith, as well as the message, of those two humble missionaries, and this led to my conversion. I suppose I'll never meet those two missionaries here in mortality, but I'll be forever grateful to them. I know not where they were from. I think one was named Fetzer."

At this point, President Burt and I looked at President Fetzer and noticed the great tears coursing down his cheeks. Without saying a word to us, President Fetzer tapped on the shoulder of the man in front of us who had just related his conversion experience. To him he then said, "I'm Bruder Fetzer. I was one of the two missionaries whom you befriended that night. I'm grateful to meet the boy who sat behind the stove—the lad who listened and who learned."

I do not remember the messages delivered during the priesthood meeting that night, but I shall never forget the faith-filled conversation that preceded the commencement of the meeting. 🌿

PHOTO CREDITS

146

INDEX